The New York Times

PUBLIC PROFILES

North Korea's Supreme Leaders

KIM IL-SUNG, KIM JONG-IL AND KIM JONG-UN

EDUCATIONAL PUBLISHING BOOKS

THE NEW YORK TIMES EDITORIAL STAFF

Published in 2019 by The New York Times® Educational Publishing in association with The Rosen Publishing Group, Inc.
29 East 21st Street, New York, NY 10010

First Edition

The New York Times
Alex Ward: Editorial Director, Book Development
Phyllis Collazo: Photo Rights/Permissions Editor
Heidi Giovine: Administrative Manager

Rosen Publishing
Megan Kellerman: Managing Editor
Jacob R. Steinberg: Editor
Greg Tucker: Creative Director
Brian Garvey: Art Director

Cataloging-in-Publication Data
Names: New York Times Company.
Title: North Korea's supreme leaders: Kim Il-sung, Kim Jong-il and Kim Jong-un / edited by the New York Times editorial staff.
Description: New York : New York Times Educational Publishing, 2019. | Series: Public profiles | Includes glossary and index.
Identifiers: ISBN 9781642821697 (library bound) | ISBN 9781642821680 (pbk.) | ISBN 9781642821703 (ebook)
Subjects: LCSH: Kim, Il-sŏng, 1912-1994—Juvenile literature. | Kim, Chŏng-il, 1942-2011—Juvenile literature. | Kim, Chŏng-ŭn, 1984—Juvenile literature. | Dictators—Korea (North)—Biography—Juvenile literature. | Heads of state—Korea (North)—Biography—Juvenile literature. | Korea (North)—Politics and government—Juvenile literature.
Classification: LCC DS934.6.K5 N678 2019 | DDC 951.9304'3'092 B—dc23

Manufactured in the United States of America

On the cover: Soldiers paying respect to Kim Il-sung; narvikk/iStock Unreleased/Getty Images.

Contents

CHAPTER 3

Grooming an Heir, Building a Dynasty

CHAPTER 4

Kim Jong-il Takes Power

Introduction

WHEN WORLD WAR II ENDED in August 1945, the Korean peninsula was left divided. Once wartime allies, the relationship between the Union of Soviet Socialist Republics and the United States quickly soured as the two nations came to represent opposing political and economic ideologies. Along the 38th parallel north, Korea was split into two zones: the Soviet-occupied North and the American-occupied South.

At the time, all parties desired a unified, independent Korea, but negotiations between the U.S.S.R. and the United States did not bear fruit. By 1948, the U.S.-occupied South held elections under the auspices of the United Nations, while the Soviet Union held its own elections in the North. On Sept. 9, 1948, the Democratic People's Republic of Korea, or North Korea, was proclaimed, with a Soviet-installed premier named Kim Il-sung as its leader.

Born in 1912, Kim had grown up first in Japanese-occupied Korea and later in Manchuria, where, as a teenager, he became influenced by communist ideology. When the Japanese began an occupation of Manchuria in 1935, Kim became a skilled guerrilla fighter and was a target of the Japanese army. He escaped to the Soviet Union, where he became a member of the Soviet army and fought with them against Japan until the end of World War II. Having impressed the Soviets, he swiftly rose to prominence in post-war North Korea.

In his first years as leader, Kim instituted reforms in labor rights, health care and land distribution. He also began to style himself as the "Great Leader," the onset of an intense personality cult that would outlive Kim himself.

In 1950, with Soviet and Chinese support, North Korea launched an offensive to occupy South Korea, hoping to reunite the two under

Kim's leadership. Though the surprise invasion allowed the North Korean forces to advance quickly, United Nations forces intervened, and after three years of fighting, Korea remained divided fairly close to its pre-war boundary.

In the decades that followed, Kim Il-sung developed his cult of personality, reaching nearly God-like status for the North Korean people. Further, he promoted an ideology known as juche, or self-reliance. A blend of communism, Korean nationalism and admiration for Kim as leader, juche remains the official state ideology of North Korea to this day.

By the 1980s, foreign observers began to note the rising prominence of Kim Il-sung's son, Kim Jong-il. The cult of Kim began to extend to the younger Kim as he was appointed to increasingly important party positions.

The 1990s were a turning point for North Korea. In 1994, Kim Il-sung died, and after a lengthy mourning period, Kim Jong-il assumed formal leadership of the country. Meanwhile, however, the collapse of the Soviet Union and the aid it exported severely harmed the North Korean economy. North Koreans faced famine, in addition to the severe political repression and state surveillance that is a hallmark of the Kim regime. Without the powerful U.S.S.R. to protect his power, Kim Jong-il began developing nuclear weapons, engaging in a diplomatic game of cat and mouse with the United States over North Korean denuclearization.

The second Kim proved an enigma to Western media, who seemed to oscillate between depictions of the leader as an eccentric, megalomaniac film buff and a dangerous threat to the international community. In the early 2000s, George W. Bush branded North Korea a member of an "axis of evil," further straining relations with the isolated state.

In 2011, Kim Jong-il died, but not without having appointed his son Kim Jong-un as his successor. Many were hopeful that the new Kim would bring about changes in North Korea, viewing a transition

KYODO NEWS/GETTY IMAGES

Three generations of the Kim dynasty are shown here. Featured from left to right are Kim Il-sung, Kim Jong-il, and Kim Jong-un.

of power as an opportunity for the country to improve diplomatic relations, denuclearize and lighten political repression.

In reality, the youngest Kim has been unpredictable. At times, he has revved up North Korea's nuclear testing, made threats toward neighboring countries and increased antagonism toward the United States. Still, in 2018, Kim Jong-un reversed course, meeting with South Korean President Moon Jae-in and U.S. President Donald J. Trump.

The Kim dynasty is unique. They resemble a royal family but rule over a communist state. Militarism and nuclearization have given them disproportionate power in international relations, all the while engaging in horrific human rights abuses and extreme political repression.

What the future holds for the Korean peninsula is uncertain, but without doubt, the Kim family's impact on North Korean history and culture is indelible. No matter which direction the hermit state now takes, the impact of the Kims will assuredly last.

CHAPTER 1

The Rise of Kim Il-sung

With the end of World War II, Korea was at last freed by U.S. and Soviet forces from four decades of Japanese rule. But the swift rise of Cold War tensions prevented the two nations from establishing a unified Korean government. Failed negotiations led to the Korean War (1950–1953), which left the peninsula even more bitterly divided than before. South Korea became a U.S. ally under a successive series of strongmen, while in the North, the Soviet-backed Kim Il-sung consolidated power, establishing communist rule and Soviet-styled economic policies.

The 38th Parallel

BY THE NEW YORK TIMES | SEPT. 29, 1945

ONE OF THE LEAST UNDERSTANDABLE of the many muddled and tragic situations that have accompanied the liberation of Korea from forty years of Japanese peonage has been the division of that small country into two zones of occupation. The Red Army occupies the rich, industrial northern half of the country, from the Manchurian border to the Thirty-eighth Parallel of latitude. United States troops occupy the agricultural section from the capital city of Seoul south to the Korean Strait.

There has been no official explanation of just when or by whom the decision was made to split Korea into two zones. In his statement promising a free Korea at the earliest possible moment President Truman spoke of the rebuilding of the country by the United States, Russia,

Britain and China, but if the latter two have had anything to say about affairs within Korea there has been no outward indication of it.

As is customary with all such divisions, differing policies govern in each zone. In the northern zone the Russians reportedly have largely turned over civil administration to the Korean Committee of Liberation, an organization of Korean Communists that was formed in Russia a year ago. In the United States zone of occupation we first had the Japanese retained in civil positions, and now, apparently, we are having an on-the-spot selection of Koreans to take over administrative posts.

The United States for years has declined to recognize any of the various exiled Korean groups as a legal government, although both China and France have recognized the Korean Provisional Government that was formed in Seoul in 1919 and maintained itself in China since that time. Its members now are cooling their heels in Chungking, unable to obtain transportation into Korea from the United States Army.

If, as rumored in Washington, Korea is to be ruled for a time as an International Trusteeship, under the formula worked out at San Francisco, then the sooner this plan is put into effect the better. That would be a hard blow to Korean hopes of early independence, but it would be better than the present division, which many persons feel is an invitation to future trouble among the Koreans themselves.

Communist Issue Growing in Korea

BY RICHARD J. H. JOHNSTON | APRIL 27, 1946

SEOUL, KOREA, APRIL 26 — Kim Il-sung, head of the Soviet-sponsored Interim Peoples Committee in North Korea, which has been acting as a "Government" in the Soviet occupation zone, arrived in Seoul today, presumably for a conference with Communist leaders here.

Cho Man-sik, head of the Democratic party in North Korea, is still under hotel arrest by the Russians. But Kim Il-sung is believed to have crossed the border at the Thirty-sixth Parallel under Soviet sponsorship.

Kim is an erstwhile "general" who, according to Koreans here, is actually an "imposter." It is held that he has been offered by the Russians to the Koreans as the now legendary Kim Il-sung, an aged leader in the fight against the Japanese, who is believed to be dead.

Kim arrived here without the knowledge of the American authorities. His arrival, plus reports of further commission decisions, added impetus to the belief that a bitter struggle between the United States and the Soviet delegations over the establishment of a Korean Government may be about to be brought into the open.

TRIP UNDER DISCUSSION

Meanwhile, the joint commission has been discussing for the last three days the question of the commission's visit to Heijo (Pyongyang), capital of the Soviet occupation zone, for consultations there with Korean groups.

It was reported that the commission might make the northward journey within a fortnight, but it was not learned whether the American press would be permitted to accompany the commission. Lieut. Gen. John R. Hodge, commanding United States forces here, has expressed his determination to press this point.

With Dr. Syngman Rhee touring the provinces of South Korea, talking with the people, and with Kim, described here as a Soviet "puppet," looming as the largest figures, a struggle between the Communists and their opponents in this zone is believed to be imminent.

With the arrival of Kim there has come also the first visual evidence of the Communists' propaganda campaign in North Korea. It is in the form of a series of photographs taken in Heijo showing posters and street decorations that feature the Soviet hierarchy.

PHOTOGRAPHS OF RUSSIANS

Huge photographs of Premier Stalin and other Soviet leaders adorn the street corners and billboards.

A number of these photographs depict signboards bearing attacks on Dr. Rhee. These posters charge that Dr. Rhee faced United States courts seven times for illegal acts in the United States and that he is at present being investigated by American authorities here. The authorities here state that such allegations have no basis in fact.

General Hodge gave to the Korean press today a clarification of the requirement of the joint commission that Korean political groups selected for consultation must sign a pledge to "uphold the aims of the Moscow decision." General Hodge declared:

> *Maj. Gen. A. V. Arnold, chief of the American delegation to the commission, confirms me in the understanding that by signing this declaration, Koreans may assure themselves of the privilege of expressing their views to the commission, either for or against trusteeship.*

North Will Demand Rule of All Korea

BY THE NEW YORK TIMES | SEPT. 1, 1948

SEOUL, KOREA, AUG. 31 — The North Korea Soviet-controlled radio has announced that the "Supreme Korean People's Assembly" will meet for the first time in Pyongyang, capital of the Russian zone, on Thursday.

Claiming to represent all Korea as a result of recent "elections" this assembly, according to the Pyongyang radio, will be the "legitimate supreme legislative organ of the central government of Korea."

The assembly will be composed of 527 representatives. Of these 360 are reported to represent South Korea.

These 360 are said to have been chosen on Aug. 25 by means of an "underground election" in South Korea.

According to the Soviet radio these elections were "held despite bitter South Korean reactionary police oppression, and resulted in a ballot of 77.48 per cent of the 8,681,745 who cast their votes. The eligible voters claimed by the Communists is nearly a million more than the total registration in South Korea for the United Nations-sponsored elections.

The Communists claim representation in proportion to the population of the two zones. Two-thirds of Korea's 29,000,000 live in South Korea.

The Communist-controlled North Korea Government, it is reported, will send a delegation to Paris to tell the General Assembly of the United Nations that it represents the true government of Korea and that the present Korean Republic set up in South Korea under United Nations observation is a fraudulent organization.

North Korea Head Calls Labor Lax

BY THE NEW YORK TIMES | NOV. 25, 1949

SEOUL, KOREA, NOV. 24 — Premier Kim Il-sung, head of the Communist-led North Korean regime, indicated on Monday that poor labor discipline, lassitude and anti-Communist sabotage were hampering industrial production in that region.

He told in blunt terms of the difficulties of getting the working class to assume the responsibilities envisaged by Communist doctrine. His remarks were made in a lengthy speech concluding the four-day conference of industrial and labor leaders in Pyongyang, seat of the North Korean Government.

Mr. Kim quoted statistics to show that North Korean production still was increasing but he said production was not what it should be.

The United States-sponsored South Korean Government has asserted it has an underground in the North, but never before has the Soviet-sponsored Government acknowledged it so frankly.

Mr. Kim said elements within the country were "bending every effort to obstruct the industrial development and consolidation of the People's State by sabotage and destruction under the South Korean reactionaries." He urged the people to vigilance "no matter how the enemy may disguise himself" and said, "We must steadily foster among the people hatred against the enemies of our People's State."

He said that when workers wrecked machinery or produced below-standard goods under the Japanese it was praiseworthy but that now plants were the property of the people, a situation "fundamentally changed." Nevertheless, he said, certain persons "fail to see the fundamental difference."

Mr. Kim, who reportedly was educated in Moscow, said workers newly thrust into executive positions often failed to live up to their responsibilities. There was a lack of "strict labor discipline" that top workers should impose on themselves as an example to their subordinates, he said. There was at many establishments "disorder and a tendency to evade individual responsibility," he added.

Other shortcomings, which he listed, were failure of industrial leaders to apply the principle of "unified administration"; reluctance of factory managers to pay workers on an individual production basis because of the tedious bookkeeping involved; failure of factories to produce a capacity amount of daily necessities.

Mr. Kim also set forth his concept of the proper function of trade unions. They must be reorganized "in the interests of the State and the people," he said. Their function, he said, should consist of the mobilization of the masses to fulfill the State program, protect State property, promote production contests and foster labor discipline.

War in Korea

BY THE NEW YORK TIMES | JUNE 26, 1950

THE SOVIETS' PUPPETS in North Korea have set the match to the powder train. The world's major concern now is whether the universal conflagration can be avoided. The United States has acted promptly and the United Nations has done likewise. Whether their action, as at present projected, will be sufficient to restore the peace is problematical.

The powder train was laid in a long series of clashes with the Soviet Union. The 38th Parallel, established initially merely as a military marker to facilitate the acceptance of Japanese surrender, was quickly turned by the Soviet Union into an impassable political barrier. Behind this barrier was established the now familiar puppet regime, and this regime was supplied with a Soviet-trained and Soviet-equipped army. The Russians, having blocked every attempt at agreement or unification, then ostentatiously withdrew their own army — or said they did — and called upon the United States to do likewise. The United States ended its occupation but had meanwhile given substantial help in the formation of a free and democratic government — installed and recognized under the express guidance and approval of the United Nations. In the United Nations the Soviet Union undertook to prevent these steps but did not succeed. Nevertheless, it prevented the entry of the lawful Government of Korea into the United Nations and has attempted at every turn to impede and discredit the young republic. These moves have also failed.

Meanwhile, for two years, a Soviet-inspired conspiracy of sabotage, infiltration, terrorism and treason has sought to destroy the Korean Government from within. This campaign also has failed, as American officials have recently testified. The next move, therefore, is frontal attack. It is obviously Soviet-authorized, but we may be sure that there will be loud disclaimers from Moscow. It will be represented as a "natural" and "spontaneous" uprising of patriotic Koreans against "imperialism." The North Koreans have already added the familiar dodge of representing their assault as a retaliation. This is Hitler's famous "counterattack with pursuit."

Neither the United States nor the United Nations, however, will be taken in by any such transparent fiction. They recognize that this is not a "local" dispute and that the peace of the world hangs on what can be done about it.

The United States, thus far, has done two things. It has dispatched some military materials to South Korea and it has taken the diplomatic initiative in getting the matter before an immediate and emergency session of the United Nations Security Council. What the materials are has not been disclosed. Whether they can be sufficient to offset the complete air superiority of the Russian-supplied North Korean forces is not yet known.

Meanwhile, the United Nations has given overwhelming support to the United States resolution branding the North Korean invasion as an act of aggression, calling for a cease-fire and a withdrawal, and asking support for South Korea and abstention of any aid to North. This is moral support for South Korea, but something more than moral support may be required.

Behind the prompt United Nations action must be, of course, the realization of the vital stake that the organization has in this issue. The lawful Korean Government is uniquely a United Nations creation. The invasion of its territory and an act of aggression against it is, in effect, an aggression against the United Nations and a direct defiance of its will and of its processes. If it cannot cope with this situation it may not survive in its present form.

Nevertheless, that coping presents some grave problems and difficulties. The Soviet Union, one of the five permanent members of the Security Council, chose to ignore the summons to the emergency session. It will obviously be the Soviet position, therefore, that any action of the body is illegal and will be disregarded by the Russians. This is another attempt at veto by walkout.

This question, however, may well be more academic than real. The Soviet Union would disregard any action of the United Nations that it did not like in any case. What is real, here, is how firmly the will of the peace-loving world can be expressed and how closely it can be united in expressing that will.

The effects of this situation on the United States will be no less far-reaching. What happens in Korea will affect every political and military position of the United States in the Pacific. If South Korea is lost to the Communists there must be an immediate revision of our defenses in respect to Japan and Alaska. The whole charter of the peace-treaty discussions will have been changed abruptly. The position of Okinawa will have been modified and its needs changed. The Philippines will appear in a different military aspect. There will have to be a decision about Formosa.

What this adds up to is that war in Korea will, in the immediate future, force upon the United States the necessity for a decisive and unequivocal policy and program in respect to Asia. Thus far we have temporized and improvised. Our time for that ran out when the North Korean tanks crossed the border. We can lose half a world, at this point, if we lose heart.

Premier of North Tells Army to Fight to End Against U.N.

BY THE NEW YORK TIMES | OCT. 11, 1950

TOKYO, OCT. 10 — Kim Il-sung, Communist Premier of North Korea, has rejected Gen. Douglas MacArthur's demand in the name of the United Nations that the North Korean troops lay down their arms and cease hostilities immediately. This was reported in a radio broadcast from the Communist capital of Pyongyang, monitored here at 8:30 this morning.

The broadcast said that Kim had ordered troops of the "People's Army" to fight to the end against the United Nations forces that were now in a general offensive.

The North Korean Premier called the United Nations police action "aggression" against his country. He appealed to the civil population in all the parts of Korea still in Communist hands to work harder to produce more arms, ammunition and military supplies to back the Red forces, and to repair communications lines smashed by the Allied air attack since the start of the war.

The Pyongyang radio gave no complete text of the Premier's statement. Quoting him directly, it said, however, that Kim had acknowledged that the United Nations troops had crossed the boundaries of North Korea, and that a "grave crisis faced the motherland."

It was the first admission from Communist sources that the Thirty-eighth Parallel, the old border between North and South Korea, had been pierced. Previous Pyongyang broadcasts had admitted only a withdrawal from Seoul and the southern perimeter by the Reds who were said to have "completed their missions and were recalled for important tasks elsewhere."

Kim promised his people "final victory" as the prize of determined resistance, the radio said.

He made the statement in answer to the "final demand" of General MacArthur yesterday.

ERIC LAFFORGUE/GAMMA-RAPHO/GETTY IMAGES

A propoganda poster of Kim Il-sung (right) and military personnel.

General MacArthur, addressing "the Premier, Government of North Korea," demanded the surrender of the "forces under your command in whatever part of Korea they are situated." Under the authority of the resolution adopted last week by the General Assembly of the United Nations, General MacArthur called upon all Koreans to cooperate in the unification of the nation under a democratic government.

REPLY WITHIN 48 HOURS

Kim's reply came less than forty-eight hours after General MacArthur's demand had been broadcast over the Tokyo and Seoul radios in Korean. It contrasted sharply with the North Korean attitude toward the general's first message of Oct. 1, making a similar demand on the Communist military high command. That message was ignored.

Since then, however, the United Nations has pushed its offensive deep within the Communist frontier to Wonsan on the east, and

American troops now are hammering at enemy defenses directly south of Pyongyang, only eighty miles away.

There was no immediate reaction in General MacArthur's headquarters to Kim's refusal to accept the United Nations authority, and it was indicated there might be no answer in words to the North Korean Premier.

General MacArthur already had informed Kim that in case of refusal, or even a lack of an immediate answer, "such military action as may be necessary to enforce the decrees of the United Nations" would he taken. This already was under way with the Allied offensive. The most convincing reply that could made to the Communist leadership, it was believed here, would be continuance of the assault in force.

Observers here expressed interest in Kim's appeal to the civil population in the north as well as the Communist soldiers. The North Korean chief apparently was answering General MacArthur's call to "all North Koreans" to cooperate with the United Nations regardless of the Communist Government's attitude.

Intelligence officers here and at the front, after having questioned thousands of prisoners, concluded that a majority of the North Korean populace had turned against the Red Government after its unsuccessful invasion attempt and its severe military and forced labor drafts. Kim, however, apparently was attempting to picture the Communist regime still as a solid national organization, to whose appeal for further sacrifices the people would listen willingly.

Observers here never had any reason to suppose that the Communist leaders in North Korea faced with possible war-crimes trials for aggression and mass executions of military prisoners and civilians, would surrender. It had been expected that in case of collapse they would flee across the border to the neighboring Communist states of China or the Soviet Union.

CHAPTER 2

The Cult of Kim

Following the Korean War, Kim Il-sung purged the Korean Workers' Party of his opponents and built a cult of personality akin to Joseph Stalin's in the Soviet Union. However, following Stalin's death, the Soviet Union came to denounce Stalin and his leadership style, which Chinese Communists still defended. The result was the Sino-Soviet split. As the world's Communist regimes chose their alliance (with either the Soviet Union or China), Kim masterfully navigated between the two, ensuring advantageous military and trade agreements for his regime.

North Korean Enigma: Kim Il-sung

BY THE NEW YORK TIMES | JULY 12, 1961

THE SLEEPY-EYED, rotund North Korean who signed a new military assistance pact with Communist China yesterday took the name of a Korean anti-Japanese guerrilla leader at a propitious moment in history.

Kim Il-sung, whose original name is Kim Sung Chu, has been the Communist leader in North Korea since August, 1945, when he rode into Pyongyang with Soviet troops under the command of Guard Col. Terentyi Fromitch Shtikov.

Mr. Kim's namesake began his one-man war against the Japanese as early as 1905, when the Japanese annexation of Korea began. As Robert Bruce was to the Scots and Robert Emmet to the Irish, so was Kim Il-sung to two generations of Koreans.

How the legendary hero died, where he is buried and how many Japanese he killed is lost in the mists of the Diamond Mountains. To Koreans he was simply a great man.

Trading upon this name came Kim Sung Chu, born in 1912 in the village of Man Gindyu, near the North Korean capital of Pyongyang. To him his supporters have attributed the deeds of the heroic Kim Il-sung, who, were he alive, would be in his mid-eighties.

STUDIED IN MOSCOW

Under Soviet tutelage, the younger Mr. Kim attended graduate and post-graduate courses in Moscow in the years before World War II. He was preparing, along with other countrymen selected by the Kremlin, for the day when Communist forces would "liberate Korea from the Imperial Japanese."

So obscure was Mr. Kim in the prewar years that he was unknown to Koreans except those in the Communist underground. For a simple farm boy, his course was carefully charted by his mentors — so carefully that there is no record of him in North Korea prior to 1945.

He first appeared bearing the name of Kim Il-sung as chairman of the People's Committee for North Korea, set up by the Soviet occupation force to give a semblance of Korean and civil authority to the occupation.

From 1945 through 1948, edicts were issued in his name from Pyongyang to the vast amusement — and increasing bewilderment — of the veterans of Korea's decades-old struggle against the Japanese colonists.

Oh Sei Chang, a venerable Korean patriot and a prime mover in the sanguinary "Sam Il" uprising against the Japanese many years before, publicly deplored the "sullying" of the name of his great compatriot.

From 1945 through the Korean war, which ended in a truce in 1953, many of Mr. Kim's fellow Korean Communists fell by the wayside for various reasons of "deviation." These included the chief Korean Communist, the late Pak Heun Yung, who was executed by the North Korean Government for "errors in judgment" during the war.

Former Communists who have defected to the South over the years have accounted for Mr. Kim's indestructibility by saying that "he never had an original thought, took an original action or quarreled with those in power."

With the establishment of the People's Democratic Republic in North Korea in 1948 — a counter-move to the establishment of the first Korean Republic in the South — he was named Premier, a post he continues to hold with a durability that has surprised much of Korea.

FAMILY LIFE UNKNOWN

It is not publicly known whether he is married or has any living relatives. No reference has ever been made, even in lengthy, laudatory accounts of his leadership from the Pyongyang radio, to a wife or children.

Frequently photographed at political gatherings, Mr. Kim is never seen, as are other Communist functionaries, with a wife or companion.

He has been called in South Korea "the remarkable man who is not." His somnolent countenance, however, is known to all Koreans. His voice has rarely been heard, his decrees rarely disobeyed. He is Soviet-oriented, but apparently is still able to do business with the Chinese.

North Korea Bids Reds Back Hanoi

BY THE NEW YORK TIMES | OCT. 6, 1966

TOKYO, OCT. 5 — Premier Kim Il-sung of North Korea urged all socialist countries today to send volunteers to Vietnam to resist the United States. He made this remark in a speech to the opening session of the North Korean Communist party conference in Pyongyang.

Mr. Kim, chairman of the party, said in the speech, which was monitored in Tokyo:

> *In the light of the situation where the U. S. imperialists are expanding aggression against the Democratic Republic of Vietnam by bringing in troops of their subordinate countries and puppets, every socialist country should dispatch volunteers to Vietnam to defend the southeastern outpost of the socialist camp.*
>
> *This is the internationalist duty of the socialist countries to the brotherly Vietnamese people. No one can oppose the socialist countries dispatching volunteers to Vietnam.*
>
> *We are preparing to send our volunteers to join the Vietnamese brother and sisters in their battle whenever requested by the Government of the Democratic Republic of Vietnam.*

DEPLORES RED DISCORD

Deploring the discord among the Communist countries created by the Soviet-Chinese split, Mr. Kim said:

> *At present the countries of the socialist camp are not keeping step with each other in opposing U. S. aggression and aiding the Vietnamese people because of differences among themselves. This afflicts the fighting people of Vietnam and really saddens us Communists.*

He stated that the differences among the Communist countries had been aggravated so much that "they have passed the ideological and theoretical limits and can hardly be settled now."

However, in expressing hope for the restoration of unity of the Communist countries, the North Korean Premier said that "relationships between the fraternal parties should in no way be considered a hostile one such as that with imperialism."

The North Korean leader said that Washington's role in Vietnam was a challenge to all the countries of the socialist camp. He emphasized the need to intensify the struggles of all socialist countries against the United States and its allies.

ANTI-TOKYO FIGHT STRESSED

"The struggle against Japanese imperialism is the struggle to defend peace in Asia and the world and is an important link in the chain of the struggle against U. S. imperialism," Mr. Kim declared.

> *Struggles should be intensified particularly against Japanese and West German militarism. We must see the danger of Japanese militarism in Asia along with that of West German militarism in Europe.*
>
> *As all the socialist countries struggle against West German militarism as well as U. S. imperialism in Europe, so they should fight against Japanese imperialism as well as U. S. imperialism in Asia.*

"Despite their discords, U. S. imperialism and Japanese imperialism are bound together by an alliance between the boss and the subordinate for the sake of their common interests in Asian aggression and are aligned with each other politically, economically and militarily," Mr. Kim continued.

"The contradictions between the United States and Japan should not be overestimated and the boss-servant alliance between the two should not be underestimated."

Korean Nationalist: Kim Il-sung

BY THE NEW YORK TIMES | JAN. 24, 1968

WASHINGTON, JAN. 23 — In the political life of Premier Kim Il-sung of North Korea, whose navy seized a United States vessel today, two facts stand out: His love of Korea and his hatred of the Japanese.

His Communism has been nationalistic, but not isolationist. He has managed to keep his lines open to Moscow and Peking, no easy feat for the leader of a small country near the two giants of Communism.

He was trained in Communist political tactics by the Soviet Union, became an officer in its army while exiled from his native land and, on his return, ruled as Stalin did — through personality and purges in the party.

Although attacked as a "revisionist" by Red Guard posters in Communist China a year ago, Premier Kim has appeared to maintain a viable relationship with China. He signed a military assistance pact with Peking in 1963.

VISITED MOSCOW IN 1959

He was last in the Soviet Union in 1959, as far as is publicly known. In the last year or so, he has sent his deputy to meetings in Moscow.

The son of a middle-class schoolmaster, he fled North Korea with his parents to avoid persecution. Although born Kim Sung-Chu, he took the name of a Korean who opposed the Japanese as early as 1905, when their annexation of Korea began.

One year of his absence from North Korea was spent in prison, his penalty for organizing anti-Japanese activity on Korea's northern borders.

He received his military and political training around 1940 in the Soviet city of Khabarovsk. He returned to North Korea in 1945 as a captain in the Soviet Army that accepted the surrender of the Japanese occupation forces.

Mr. Kim obtained control of the Communist party of Korea and, in 1946, absorbed the New Peoples party, composed of Chinese-trained party leaders.

The first purge took place in the winter of 1946-47. The present regime was formed in 1948.

Mr. Kim, who holds the title of Secretary General of the Korean Workers' party as well as Premier, was born on April 15, 1912, in Mang Yong Dae. He was married in Manchuria during his years in exile. His wife, who bore him two sons, died in 1949.

In 1950 he married the daughter of the head of the former South Korean National Independence Federation, whose function was to bring left-wing national parties under Communist control.

North Korea Says the World Hails Kim Il-sung

BY THE NEW YORK TIMES | NOV. 25, 1969

HONG KONG, NOV. 24 — North Korea has described full-page advertisements inserted in The New York Times and The Times of London, as "articles" in a Pyongyang report implying that the world's press has acclaimed a biography of Premier Kim Il-sung.

The report, transmitted abroad by the official North Korean press agency and monitored here, said that publications of many capitalist countries, including the United States, Britain, Sweden and Japan, were "widely introducing" a biography of Premier Kim, "the respected and beloved leader of the 40 million Korean people, a great Marxist-Leninist and one of the outstanding leaders of the international Communist movement and working class movement."

A full-page advertisement appeared in The New York Times on Oct. 27 announcing the publication in English of a biography of Kim Il-sung by the Miraisha Company of Tokyo. A similar advertisement appeared in The London Times on Nov. 3.

'HERO OF THE CENTURY'

The Pyongyang report said that "under the block-letter title, 'Korea Has Produced the Hero of the 20th Century' " The New York Times had "allocated one whole page to an article introducing the English edition of the first volume of the biography of Kim Il-sung."

"The paper gave a detailed description of the revolutionary family and early revolutionary activities of Comrade Kim Il-sung, the great leader, and his brilliant history of revolutionary struggles, sagacity of leadership and lofty virtues during the anti-Japanese armed struggle," the agency said.

Learning from The New York Times that the biography had "come off the press in English at last," progressive people and "public circles"

NICK LEDGER/AWL IMAGES/GETTY IMAGES

A wall mural depicts the return of Kim Il-sung to Pyongyang at the end of World War II.

in the United States have ardently desired to obtain the book, the agency said.

Though the biography was printed in Japan and the advertisements were arranged from Tokyo, there has been speculation that the financing came from North Korea. The South Korean Foreign Ministry has made representations to the United States and British Governments, expressing concern over publication of the advertisements.

A Visit to North Korea

BY ALAIN BOUC | JUNE 14, 1971

PYONGYANG, NORTH KOREA — No country wants to be autonomous as much as North Korea, and that is sensed instantly. As soon as the visitor leaves the plane, he enters into an unknown political universe, dominated by the alternately austere and relaxed figure of Kim Il-sung, Chief of State, Prime Minister, Secretary General of the Worker's party, "national hero," "hero of the 20th century," "invincible patriot," "leader of forty million Koreans."

The young women of the pioneer movement, who present crowns of flowers, are dressed in the colors of the flag, red and blue. The clear shades of the national costume — long, pale blue or light red dresses, are worn by all the women and contrast with their black hair.

A feeling of independence stems from the beautiful, well-irrigated rice paddies, worked on by tractor, which allow each person 800 grams of grain per day — more than they can consume. Pyongyang radio never fails regularly to offer surplus cereals to the South, in order to force Seoul into a refusal that is easily exploitable along the theme: "The fanatic South Koreans prefer American surplus to the rice of their own country."

I rolled along, at a rapid pace, toward Pyongyang in a Soviet vehicle, but all the vehicles I encountered were constructed in this country — from bicycles to tractors, wagons, buses.

Those who have seen East Berlin and Stalin Allee will have an idea of what Pyongyang looks like. The living units are poorer than they appear to be, but are aligned in the same manner along great avenues where the traffic is scarcely intense. North Korea is not rich, but it is proud and clean. In Pyongyang, as in the center of the smallest villages, flowers abound in the flower beds, after three months of snow. The lawns are cut, the sewers are cleaned out. The children of the villages plow the fields, dressed like townsmen. The same discipline, the same watchwords in the country and the city. The small, rural homes with gray and white tile roofs, can even appear gayer than the great houses of unornamented reinforced concrete in the principal urban areas.

Independence and autonomy are more apparent when one travels to the factories. The small, Japanese nucleus provided some manpower. But, they now work on North Korean machines and tools in order to produce equipment used in the country, and to strengthen national economic power. There are many women working in precision mechanics, and they are supposedly better than the men. The men are dominant in the great metallurgy enterprises, and the activism of the workers of the blast furnaces sets an example for the rest of the country.

In what atmosphere does this national Communism of Korea develop? The climate is certainly tense, but one would not call it oppressive. No idlers, street peddlers, useless occupations. From 6 A.M. the wagons loaded with workers and with women workers behind, always singing, pass in front of my hotel, on the public square of the great theater, in the direction of the factories and the dockyards. Lines form at the bus stops. Groups of children, singing the hymn of Kim Il-sung, go to school. The passersby move in decided steps, neither running nor sauntering, under the weeping willows, along the river and in the parks, young men and women study technical matters more than literature, politics more than international geography, and the works of Kim Il-sung more than those of Marx or of Mao Tse-tung.

Premier's Presence Blankets Pyongyang

BY HARRISON E. SALISBURY | MAY 17, 1972

PYONGYANG, NORTH KOREA, MAY 16 — In the entrance hall to Pyongyang's Kim Il-sung University there is a large statue of Korea's leader. On the second floor there is a sequence of 10 separate rooms, each devoted to a phase of the Premier's life and achievements, particularly those pertaining to the university. And the visitor is informed that the university was founded personally by the Premier on Oct. 3, 1946.

The visitor to North Korea quickly notices the pervasive presence of Premier Kim Il-sung in a picture or statue at almost every turn. And at each institution the visitor is told of the Premier's personal interest and solicitude for every variety of public, social and state enterprise.

'OUR BELOVED LEADER'

The Premier is customarily referred to by every official as "our beloved and respected leader, Comrade Kim Il-sung." The Premier has visited the university 80 times and has issued 220 guidance directives on university affairs. Each of these visits and directives is depicted for the enlightenment of students and faculty in the 10 rooms devoted to his life.

The care with which the university cherishes the memory of his visits and interventions is not unique. The Pyongyang Children's Palace, also founded by the Premier, displays a similar respect for the leader in a room in which young boys are taught to drive trucks. A plaque notes that Premier Kim Il-sung has visited the room six times.

The date of each visit is also recorded at the Mangyongdae State Hatchery, a mechanized egg-producing operation that the director, Jyong Ryon Kim, said had been "built under the solicitude of our beloved and respected leader, Comrade Kim Il-sung."

ASSOCIATED PRESS

A statue of Kim Il-sung at Kim Il-sung University in Pyongyang.

A plaque in the elevator quotes the words of the Premier. "In order to improve the people's living standard it is essential to produce more eggs at a lower price." This is a task to which the hatchery is said to have successfully applied itself last year, by turning out more than 100 million eggs.

Kim Il-sung University is an imposing institution with an enrollment of more than 10,000 students and a staff and faculty of 3,000. About 2,000 students are graduated each year.

The school library is said to contain more than one million volumes, including the complete works of the Premier, in Korean and translated into dozens of foreign languages. Few students or scholars were at work in the modern library building today. But this was explained by the fact that the regular school year has ended for most of the students and they are now doing what is called "practical work" in the fields and factories.

SKYSCRAPER BEING BUILT

A 22-story campus building is nearing completion. When the whole university building project is finished — this is expected by 1976 — the facilities should be the envy of many American colleges.

The blueprints for the new university buildings have been approved by the Premier.

One of the most striking demonstrations of the Premier's interest in the university is to be found in its museum of natural history. It is filled with exhibits donated by the Premier. There are 120 examples of birds, animals and fish, all sent by him.

He has even donated his fine-tooled shotgun, which he gave in 1953 with the suggestion that if the museum needed more subjects for research it use the gun to obtain them.

The exhibition includes a pet black bear, which the Premier kept at home until he sent it to the university in 1948. It was reportedly killed during the war by an American bomb, and now is mounted in the exhibit along with the Premier's hunting dog, a setter. There is also a mounted fish that the Premier caught in 1958. Specialists at the university have been unable to determine its species.

On Aug. 5, 1961, the Premier presented the university with a large eel and last March he donated a huge boar that he said had been given to him by a peasant.

On April 3, 1962, he gave the university an albino sea cucumber and on Feb. 3, 1963, a pheasant that appears to have both male and female characteristics. In February, 1971, he donated a 900-pound black hear. The university roasted the meat after having stuffed the skin and every student at the university received a piece of bear meat.

In 1959, the Premier gave the exhibit a sparrow that he had kept and fed at home, and in February, 1970, a pair of ducks. As the deputy rector noted, it is small wonder "that our students call him our fatherly leader." A similar sentiment was expressed by Moung Suk Kim, the director of ideology at the Children's Palace, who said, "Now all our children are living warmly in the deep bosom of our leader, Kim Il-sung."

Excerpts From Interview With North Korean Premier on Policy Toward the U.S.

BY THE NEW YORK TIMES | MAY 31, 1972

Following are excerpts from an interview conducted with Premier Kim Il-sung through an official interpreter by Harrison E. Salisbury and John M. Lee of The New York Times:

PREMIER KIM: You wrote me many times asking to come so I let you. It is 10 years after your first application, but my secretary told me that you did not have a very good impression because of the strong anti-American expressions of the Korean people.

It is inevitable that we Koreans have bad sentiments toward Americans. We had very difficult contacts with Americans. It is also the first time for me to meet Americans in several scores of years.

Actually our country is still in a state of cease-fire. No peace treaty has yet been concluded, has it? Virtually we are still in a state of cease-fire and we have not yet settled the question by peaceful means, have we?

Therefore I always say our generations are changing but the target of our struggle remains the same.

There are many reasons here. As you already know, even after the armistice, the U.S. Government still adopts unfriendly attitudes toward our country. Under these circumstances we cannot but prepare ourselves always for war.

The most important thing in war preparation, in my opinion, is that we educate our people in the spirit of hating the enemy. Without educating our people in this spirit we cannot defeat the U.S., which is superior in technology.

Therefore, we frankly tell you we are always making preparations for war. We do not conceal this matter. We are making preparations openly. Nobody can tell, neither you nor I can tell, what time you'll pounce upon us. Therefore, I think it is quite natural and quite all right to educate people with the spirit of hating the target of our struggle.

WIDESPREAD SUFFERING CITED

I do not think there is any Korean who has not suffered in the Korean war. At least relatives or friends of all of us suffered. Tens of thousands of people were killed by indiscriminate bombings. In Pyongyang alone all houses were reduced to ashes and only three houses were left intact. Not only Pyongyang but also Wonsan and Hamhung and others, and then by the end of the war, all our villages were destroyed indiscriminately. In these circumstances, we Koreans can have nothing but bad sentiments toward Americans.

Under the armistice agreement it was promised that parties concerned in the war should conclude a peace between the North and the South so that peace might be brought to Korea. But the U.S. authorities do not keep their promise.

In recent years, after the Pueblo incident, the U.S. authorities conducted reconnaissance over our country by high-altitude reconnaissance planes.

In this way we are in a state of war. So we cannot but devote more funds to strengthening our defensive power and this, frankly speaking, affects the increase in the living standards of our people to a certain extent.

We always say this is only because of the U.S.

We not only suffered from the war, but after the war we are in a state of war. U.S. authorities violate the armistice agreement and adopt unfriendly attitudes toward us and conduct reconnaissance against our country.

And we educate our people on this, and therefore our people cannot but have bad feelings against Americans. You must understand things in this way.

ISSUE IS PUT TO THE U.S.

Q: *What positive steps should be taken to end the abnormal state of relations between the United States and Korea?*

A: From our point of view it is very simple. Everything entirely depends on the United States Government. If the United States Government changes its policy toward us we will also change ours toward it. The most important thing is to leave the Koreans to unify their country by themselves and not interfere in the internal affairs of the Korean people.

Nearly 20 years have passed since the signing of the armistice agreement, and what kind of necessity do you have for stationing forces in South Korea under the signboard of the United Nations forces?

Some people say you are staying in South Korea to protect the South Koreans because we want to invade South Korea. But we have declared time and time again we have no intention at all of invading South Korea. Therefore I think it is high time for you to put an end to your role of police. If you withdraw we Koreans can do things in common for peaceful unification.

What the United States Government does that displeases us is not only station its troops in South Korea but helps the revival of Japanese militarists. So we see the joint communiqué of 1969 between Nixon and Sato, and Nixon put forward the so-called Nixon Doctrine under which he instigated Japanese militarists so as to replace the United States in South Korea so as to interfere in the internal affairs of the Korean people.

After the joint communique Sato claimed he would interfere in the internal affairs of the Korean question. We cannot but describe this as an unfriendly attitude of the United States Government toward us.

The American attitude toward us at the United Nations is not justified either. Why do they attach conditions to inviting us to the United Nations while they invite the South Koreans without any conditions? They insisted we recognize the legality of the resolutions adopted at the United Nations against us. How can we go under such preconditions?

And you also instigate the so-called United Nations Commission for the Unification and Rehabilitation of Korea to make an annual report full of lies and falsifications against our country and make unfriendly false propaganda.

You should withdraw United States forces, dissolve the United Nations Commission for the Unification and Rehabilitation of Korea and not encourage the division of the Korean nation but help the reunification. If there is no interference of outside forces, the Koreans can seek common points for unification of the country.

When President Nixon visited China, he said while looking at the Great Wall of China that there should be no divided countries — no barriers. If the United States Government wants to put this into practice, it must begin with Korea.

President Nixon said he wanted to improve relations with China, and while visiting the Soviet Union he said he wants to have improved relations with the Soviet Union. We say, why should he continue to have military bases in South Korea and the Korean peninsula?

If in the past you said you needed military bases in South Korea to prevent the expansion of Communism, now that you have good relations with the big powers, why is there any necessity of having military bases in South Korea?

What can you benefit by asking Japan to replace the United States in South Korea to invade South Korea and turn South Korea into a market for Japanese goods and turning it into an appendage of Japan?

The Korean nation is a single nation. We must unify this nation.

Many North Koreans have relations in South Korea and many South Koreans have relations in North Korea, So we should remove this barrier of long standing and eradicate the tragedy of Korea.

Our policy toward the United States is as follow: If the United States Government stops its unfriendly attitude toward us and stops obstructing the unification of our country, then there is no reason why we should have hostile attitudes toward the United States. So I should say relations between ourselves and the United States entirely depend on the United States and not on us.

OUTSIDERS' ROLE EXCLUDED

Q: *Is there any role in this question for outside powers such as China and the Soviet Union, or must it be solved only by the United States and Korea?*

A: In my opinion, China and the Soviet Union have very little concern with the question of Korean unification. The Soviet Union and China support the peaceful unification of Korea. I think the Korean question must be left to the Koreans to solve by themselves without any interference by outside forces on the basis of national self-determination. Only in this way can be solved in a peaceful way.

Q: *Is there any possibility that Geneva-type conference would be helpful in solving the Korean question?*

A: In my opinion, we don't need such thing. United States troops must be withdrawn first of all. Even if they are withdrawn we will not fight each other.

If Koreans are united they can keep Japan from reinvading our country. In regard to unification, Koreans can achieve agreement on common points and unification.

As you know, we have made contacts with South Korea through the North-South Red Cross talks. Of course we have to wait and see what will be the prospect of these talks and what will become of it. But we think that if North and South Koreans can sit down together they can remove present misunderstandings and distrust.

So far, because we do not sit down together, there are still frozen sentiments between us and distrust and misunderstanding in many aspects. We sit down together, we can remove all of this.

In what aspects are there misunderstandings? I think there are some. For our part we understand that South Korean rulers may invade us with the backing of the Japanese and the United States. And South Koreans misunderstand us, thinking we would invade South Korea.

Recently we hear South Koreans also want to reunify the country by independent means. They also advocate self-help, self-sustenance and self-defense. We also advocate independence, self-reliance and self-defense. These are the common points. If we develop these common points, we think we can come to an agreement uniting us.

They are also kicking up an anti-Communist racket saying we want to communize South Korea, We have no intention whatsoever of imposing socialist system on South Korea. We think it is not necessary for them to change the social system built up here for another social system.

Some foreign journalists write there are two poles in Korea — North Korea is a Communist society and South Korea is a capitalist society and these two poles cannot meet each other. They say if these two poles meet each other war will break out.

In my opinion we cannot see South Korea as a big capitalist country. Are there any big monopolies in South Korea? We don't think there are any big monopolies in South Korea. If there are, they are comprador capitalists [Korean agents for foreign businesses]. Of course we are against comprador capitalists because they obstruct the development of the national economy.

We are not against capitalism and medium and small-size enterprises in South Korea. Of course we can say South Korea is just starting to take the road of capitalism, or is just sympathizer with capitalism or is being infiltrated by capitalism or worshiping capitalism or something like that. Of course there are differences of ideals and beliefs between us. But we think we must rise above them for the sake of national unity. Since we do not impose our social system on South Korea and if they don't force us to change our social system for another social system, then these things cannot be the reasons why we do not achieve national unity.

If we establish this principle of not imposing social systems on each other, then there is no necessity for fighting each other by force of arms because neither side imposes upon the other.

It is possible that a country may have various systems and maybe people who have different kinds of beliefs. What kind of political system there should be in South Korea should be decided by the South Korean people themselves. So we see that even after unification there may be this or that political system in Korea and people who have different political beliefs may live together. Here mutual trust and respect are necessary. So in my opinion there are no conditions why we cannot unify our country.

In my speech of Aug. 6 last year, I proposed we could hold talks even with the Republican party of South Korea, the ruling party there. This comes out of our intention for mutual respect. So I think that if we achieve national unity in this way, we can eliminate mutual misunderstandings and distrust gradually and achieve the unification of our country independently and in a democratic way.

Of course it may need quite a long time. But we can unify the country on these principles.

LOW-LEVEL EXCHANGES

Q: *With what practical steps would this evolve?*

A: We demand such things — mail, visits and trade. We advocate mail exchange, mutual visits, exchange of trade and cooperation in economic development and so on. We also advocate mutual exchange of parliamentarians, scientists, as well as political figures.

We also advocate holding political negotiations between political parties and social organizations in North and South Korea. We also propose that parliamentary members of North and South Korea sit down together and hold consultations with open hearts.

For our part, we are always ready to do these things. But I wonder in what respects they are not ready to do so.

While holding North-South Red Cross talks with us, they are oppressing people demanding peaceful unification. They proclaimed the so-called state of national emergency under the fictitious pretext of a southward threat from the North.

In South Korea alone, parliamentary members from the New Democratic party and the Republican party cannot talk even among themselves. They hold so-called conferences for prevailing over Communism and are kicking up an anti-Communist racket.

All these things show they have no intention of reunifying the country. Those advocating prevailing over Communism to reunify the country mean they want to reunify the country after wiping out the Communists. How is possible to do so?

All these acts are meant to separate from each other, not to approach each other. We do not think this is a good thing.

We are dealing with this problem with patience. So we are continuing our efforts to create opportunities for contact.

Q: *Do you envisage separate social systems in the same country with gradually increasing contacts as time goes on, somewhat in the manner as has been proposed by North Vietnam and the National Liberation Front?*

A: Yes, that is the general idea. I do not know about Vietnam but our demands are just as I told you. And all these things are included in our eight-point program for unification of the country.

We propose that a confederation of North and South Korea would be all right if we can't reunify the country right away. This means forming a Supreme National Committee to consult and discuss matters of common concern for the nation while retaining different social systems intact in North and South Korea. Even now we want economic cooperation. So we think if we give South Korea what they have not and if they give us what we have not, we can develop our economy faster in exchanging in that way. So we think we must proceed from the interests of the nation.

We propose an exchange of trade, economics, culture, and scientists. We propose political negotiations on broad basis and meetings between parliamentary members on a broad basis.

They have closed their doors, not we. We are not afraid of capitalist influence coming in. We are not afraid of it because there is no reason why we should fear it. Everything will be solved if South Korea opens its door.

What if they shut the door continuously, then Japanese capitalists will come into South Korea and South Korea will be subjected to Japan economically. We do not forget history.

We know that in 1894 Japan began invading South Korea under the pretext of protecting Japanese residents in South Korea and from that time on, Korea began falling into a Japanese colony. We do not want to become Japanese colony again.

'UNPLEASANT FEELINGS'

Q: *Can there be moves to reduce tension and increase understanding between our two countries before United States withdrawal from South Korea — that is, by exchanges of journalists, cultural groups and so on?*

A: To say frankly, I wonder what kind of interesting things Americans will come here with. I don't think we can find anything interesting if we go there. It doesn't mean we want to shut the door. But so long as the basic problem is unsolved, nobody will benefit from it.

Since you have come here, you also feel unpleasant feelings. If more Americans come here and go back with unpleasant feelings, one will not benefit by it. So long as the policy is not changed, you will always feel unpleasant sentiments here and you will not benefit by it, don't you think so?

You also say you feel unpleasant here. Is it any good if we cause more people to have bad feelings here? Only when the United States Government changes its policies toward us may we discuss anti-

American sentiments and only then will it be interesting for both of us to visit each other.

So in my opinion, while the United States Government makes no big change in policy toward our country at present, I am not against mutual visits between us just on a limited scale, as at present.

Q: *This is an era of great changes in world relationships, the United States, China and the Soviet Union. Yet big problems like Korea and Vietnam remain. Do you see any hope that the changes among the big powers will positively affect the smaller powers?*

A: The United States Government should improve relations not only with the big powers but with the small powers. I don't think improved relations of the big powers will affect relations with small powers. If the United States has changed its policy in relation to China and the Soviet Union, I don't think they need military bases in South Korea any more. And if they don't need them, they must show this by practice.

If they withdraw their forces from South Korea, then it would help Koreans to harmonize with each other and will help us improve our sentiments toward the United States.

We clearly remember all the speeches made by President Nixon in China. What interests me most is Nixon said the world should not be divided and countries should not be divided when he looked up at the Great Wall of China. So I am watching with great interest what channel his words will take in practice.

Q: *What are the prospects for improving your relations with Japan?*

A: That also depends on the Japanese Government. Of course successive cabinets of the government have adopted unfriendly attitudes toward us — Yoshida, Ikeda, Kishi, Sato and all the successors.

The smaller a country is the greater the confidence and self-respect it must have. Small countries live on self-reliance and self-respect. Without self-respect, how can we live?

Absolute Ruler of North Korea

BY JOHN M. LEE | MAY 31, 1972

PYONGYANG, NORTH KOREA, MAY 26 — Portraits usually show him as dour and unsmiling, but Premier Kim Il-sung is an extroverted, even charismatic, man.

MAN IN THE NEWS

Even while wielding absolute authority, he exudes bonhomie with many broad smiles and gestures. He punctuates his sentences with little chuckles. He is a big, burly man, 60 years old, with a rolling walk, heavy-rimmed glasses and a large lump or swelling at the back of his neck. He smokes frequently but is said to refrain from drinking.

Perhaps the most striking feature of North Korea is the embodiment of the state in the life and person of this extraordinary man.

The nation abounds in perhaps the world's highest density of stone busts, bronze statues, portraits, photographs and pastel paintings of the national leader.

GIVES PERSONAL GUIDANCE

Visitors are in North Korea hardly a day before they begin hearing about "on-the-spot guidance."

These are the occasions when Premier Kim tours the Hungnam fertilizer factory or the University of the People's Economy or the Ryongsong engineering plant or Kim Il-sung University or seemingly every factory, farm or school in the country and personally orders automation, corrects the text books, draws lines in the dirt for machine emplacements, improves the students' food or picks the site for expansion.

Not all the guidance is extraordinary — his instruction recorded above the elevator at the Mangyondae chicken-raising factory reads in part: "Produce more eggs at a lower price." But it is all recorded in detail with on-the-spot photographs and displays, with the words often inscribed in red Korean characters chiseled into limestone markers.

The peasants at Chongsanri cooperative farm boast that he has given them on-the-spot guidance 62 times.

It seems rather overdone until one meets the Premier and realizes that he is just the sort of man who loves traveling around the country and involving himself in everything that is going on and telling everyone what to do.

"By meeting and talking with the masses," he said recently, "I learn of shortcomings in what we are doing. No good ideas come from sitting down in Pyongyang all the time."

The saga depicted in the various monuments to Mr. Kim, begins with revolutionary instruction in his childhood, when Japan occupied Korea. It continues through his leadership of anti-Japanese guerrillas in Manchurian border areas in the nineteen-thirties and on to his assumption of power after Korean liberation in 1945, the inconclusive clash with United States forces in the Korean war of 1950-53 and the subsequent building of a strong and hard-nosed Communist state.

SOME DETAILS IN DOUBT

His claim to revolutionary leadership is propagated in museums and countless displays devoted exclusively to his exploits. No other national figure is named outside his immediate family. His personal life, his voluminous theoretical works and his moral example form the backbone of the educational system to a degree unsurpassed in Mao Tse-tung's China or Stalin's Soviet Union.

Some details are skeptically regarded in the West, including such fundamentals as the Premier's real identity. There was a confusing name change, and the record is unaccountably fragmentary, even in Pyongyang, for the period 1941-45.

The assumption in the West is that he was in Siberia with the Russians. He reappeared in August, 1945, with the victorious Soviet Army and under its sponsorship he took command of the Communist state north of the 38th Parallel.

When the Democratic People's Republic of Korea was proclaimed on Sept. 9, 1948, he was elected Premier and has held the post ever since.

In retrospect the Russians may wonder if they picked the wrong man. Since the mid-nineteen-fifties Mr. Kim has pursued an increasingly nationalistic, independent and self-reliant policy that threads its way between the Soviet Union and China.

PATH FAR FROM SMOOTH

North Korea's development has been far from smooth. There have been party dissidents, backsliders and incompetents to be dealt with. The recent seven-year economic plan took 10 years to fulfill. But the Premier has so far come out on top in the power struggles that have raged at least as late as the mid-nineteen-sixties.

Today, Premier Kim is extravagantly acclaimed. Almost invariably he is referred to as "the respected and beloved leader" and local newspapers go on to hail him as the "peerless patriot, ever-victorious, iron-willed, brilliant commander and one of the outstanding leaders of the international Communist movement."

In kindergartens the pupils sing "There is a small hut in Mangyondae where our fatherly leader was born" — on April 15, 1912.

The record shows the youth moving to Manchuria with his family at the age of 13 and only a year later organizing the Down With Imperialism Union, disseminating Marxism-Leninism among youths and students and setting out to liberate his country.

According to a book published here, the Premier met his first wife, Kim Jong Suk, in 1936 in a southern Manchurian forest where she was a cook at a guerrilla base. She later died of tuberculosis. His second wife, Kim Sung Ae, was his secretary and is chairman of the Women's League.

FAMILY RELATIONS

Korean officials say the Premier has many children. Western sources speak of two children by the first wife and three by the second.

Last year the Premier installed his 49-year-old younger brother, Kim Yong Ju, as party secretary. Although he is nominally No. 6 in the hierarchy, outside analysts say he is an effective No. 2 and they see a dynasty in the making.

However, Premier Kim, who is just past the customary retirement age of 60, obviously has no intention of stepping down. A new slogan proclaimed a few years ago reads "60 years old — adolescence; 90 — retirement."

CHAPTER 3

Grooming an Heir, Building a Dynasty

In the late 1970s, North Korean observers noticed subtle indications that Kim Il-sung was grooming an heir: his son, Kim Jong-il. The younger Kim was appointed to increasingly important positions in the Workers' Party and came to be publicly celebrated on the same scale as his father. Nepotism was not uncommon in other Communist nations, but direct inheritance of the top leadership position was a novelty. A lengthy mourning period followed the elder Kim's death, after which he was enshrined in the constitution as "eternal President."

Son of North Korean Leader Taking a New Step Up

BY HENRY SCOTT STOKES | AUG. 10, 1980

PYONGYANG, NORTH KOREA — The Communist nation of North Korea, a perennial worry for the United States because of its aggressive attitude toward South Korea, has reached a pivotal stage in which the governing elite is orchestrating a transfer of some authority to the son of President Kim Il-sung.

President Kim, 68 years old, whose face appears on small cameo badges worn by every North Korean on suit or dress, is evidently preparing to hand over more power to his virtually unknown son,

39-year-old Kim Jong-il. Ranking North Korean officials said that in October, during the first congress of the North Korean Workers Party in 10 years, the son will inherit his father's title of Secretary General.

"It is my personal hope that Kim Jong-il will be given the position of Secretary General," an official said in a conversation in a Pyongyang park. The impression was that the matter had already been informally decided.

SOME BELIEVE POWER IS SHARED

According to Western analysts, Kim Il-sung's authority, contrary to a widespread impression abroad, is shared with other officials at the head of the two-million-member party. He is not a deity, as his cult suggests, and may even be manipulated by officials around him.

This conclusion is consistent with the observations of American intelligence officers. "Our impression is that North Korea is run by an elite of top officials, not by the Kims," an American analyst said recently in South Korea. "And it appears that it is they who may be pushing up the son to succeed the father."

The impression that this country of 19 million is wholly dominated by Kim Il-sung has been fostered in part by the South Korean Central Intelligence Agency. Agency analysts have often described him also as unstable and likely to launch a sudden attack on the South similar to that of June 25, 1950, which started the three-year Korean War.

SON VIEWED IN SEOUL AS HARD-LINER

As for his probable successor, South Korean analysts say that Kim Jong-il, President Kim's only known surviving son, graduated from Kim Il-sung University in 1963 after training as a pilot in East Germany and that he is an extreme hard-liner, more rigid even than his father. Hostile commentators in Seoul accused Kim Jong-il of responsibility for an incident in 1976 in which two United States officers were killed with axes by North Korean guards at the truce camp at Panmunjom.

In Pyongyang the younger Mr. Kim is depicted as an able moderate whose main interest is culture, serving as director of a major archaeological excavation at the town of Kangso and as the main supporter of a light opera, "The Song of Paradise," the theme of which is the peaceful construction of North Korea.

The key, and perhaps unanswerable, question for the moment is how responsive Kim Jong-il would be to the advice of a new generation of technicians who appear to favor moderation and caution though remaining nationalistic and hostile to the United States as long as almost 40,000 American soldiers are in South Korea.

ALREADY A POLITBURO MEMBER

According to officials here, Kim Jong-il is a member of the ruling Politburo and one of the party's national secretaries, who run the day-to-day affairs of North Korea. In seven or eight years he has risen swiftly in a hierarchy of much older men.

Kim Il-sung, who took over from Soviet administrators when the North Korean Government was formed in 1948, remains President and Supreme Commander of the Armed Forces. With the party, the army is a vital center of authority, holding about half of the 10 highest positions in the Politburo.

The succession of the President's son was clearly arranged years in advance in Pyongyang, and the process will apparently continue well into the 1980's.

Arranging the succession does not appear to have been an easy task for the officials concerned, given the predominance of older men in the Politburo. Many are veterans of the Manchurian guerrilla movement that fought the Japanese during the 1930's. Most of them, old companions in arms of President Kim, are near 70 and none are younger than 65, according to a ranking of the top 10 by South Korean sources.

CAUTIOUS PROCEDURE FOLLOWED

In nudging Kim Jong-il upward without naming him openly, North

Korean propaganda officials, among whom he himself is said to be prominent, refer to him in print by the code name "Party Center," an indication of the gingerly way in which the matter is being handled. So far there are no official portraits of him in public to place alongside the omnipresent ones of his father.

For outsiders there is still no certainty about his character. Officials here simply credit him with "proven ability," saying that his rise "should not be seen as a case of father following son, the creation of a ruling family."

The younger Mr. Kim must decide whether to pursue an aggressive policy or to devote an increasing share of North Korean resources to domestic development. North Korea's ultimate objectives are not clear. After a sharp rise in the number of North Korean-inspired incidents on the border in 1967 and 1968, an attempt to infiltrate guerrillas into Seoul to assassinate President Park Chung Hee of South Korea and years of increased military spending, the North Koreans changed their military strategy.

With the economy buckling, military spending was cut back sharply in 1972, apparently from 30 percent to 17 percent of the national budget. Military outlays are now said to be at a low of 14.5 percent annually, equivalent to $1.5 billion, about half the South Korean level.

At the same time tensions between North and South remain high and there has been no retreat in Pyongyang, rhetorically at least, from the basic objective of accomplishing "peaceful reunification" of the two countries. In practice this could mean reunification by any means, including the use of massive force or of covert operations aimed at exploiting the considerable domestic tension in the South.

With armed forces estimated by United States intelligence officials last year at close to 700,000 — though a top official here said that the actual size was 300,000 to 350,000 at most — the North Korean leaders appear to have at their disposal a military machine that is also markedly superior to that of the South in terms of the number of tanks and aircraft, many supplied by the Soviet Union.

President Kim, whose country has a population less than half that of the South, denies that. "We are in a state of inferiority to the South in all areas," he said in a meeting with Representative Stephen J. Solarz, Democrat of Brooklyn, who paid a four-day visit here in mid-July. "Therefore there is no reason to fear a southward invasion by us."

However, the latest American estimates comparing the 600,000-strong South Korean forces with a northern strength of 700,000 are believed to be based on careful intelligence work. The North is also said to have trained special strike forces with light aircraft, to permit the landing of guerrillas in a territory that is strongly anti-Communist and unlikely to offer significant support to infiltrators.

South Koreans, including opposition politicians, doubt that the North Koreans would use such strike forces in any large numbers. "I don't see that there is an imminent threat of an all-out attack from the North at present," Kim Dae Jung, the now-imprisoned opposition leader, commented some time ago. "Kim Il-sung will take a lesson from Indochina and not repeat his failure in the Korean War, that of all-out attack."

This reporter has not been able to confirm with North Korean officials that the North was responsible for recent incidents of infiltration by boat or clashes along the demilitarized zone at the border between North and South.

President Kim himself denied the charges and refused to respond to proposals offered by Representative Solarz for true demilitarization of the demilitarized zone, into which both sides are believed to have brought weapons; for joint observer teams in the zone, as provided in the 1953 armistice agreement that ended the Korean War, and for joint teams to repair markers designating the military demarcation line.

Mr. Solarz's unofficial effort to diminish tensions and reduce the possibility of another war in Korea thus met with little success. President Kim also declined to take up proposals he had made for mutual reductions in forces by the two Koreas or to indicate that if the United States was to withdraw its forces from South Korea, he would be willing to sign a nonaggression pact with the South.

North Korea Leader Plans Huge Fete for Son

BY HENRY SCOTT STOKES | MARCH 17, 1982

SEOUL, SOUTH KOREA, MARCH 14 — Kim Il-sung, the North Korean leader, is preparing a lavish celebration of his 70th birthday next month to pave the way for his son's succession to the leadership, according to South Korean intelligence sources.

Mr. Kim, who has led North Korea since 1945, has already delegated much authority to his 40-year-old son, Kim Jong-il, the intelligence sources said. The high point of the mammoth birthday ceremony on April 15, they said, will be the public appearance of the son at his father's side in front of an audience of 100,000 that will include dignitaries from China, the Soviet Union and the third world.

"Almost the entire North Korean Cabinet is in orbit right now," said a spokesman for the South Korean Agency for National Security Planning, an intelligence group. "They are traveling in Africa, Central and Latin America and elsewhere, seeking to drum up support." The sources said that the ministers were offering to charter aircraft to bring guests to Pyongyang, the North Korean capital, if they could not otherwise afford to travel.

The preparations for the birthday events, said the intelligence sources, include a nationwide refurbishing and polishing of some 30,000 statues and monumental busts of President Kim, including the 70-foot-high statue of the North Korean leader in Pyongyang.

SON GIVEN TITLE OF 'HERO'

A crash program is under way to complete state projects to honor the "Great Leader," as Mr. Kim is universally called in North Korea, and to show respect to "Hero Kim Jong-il." The title of "Hero" was bestowed by the father on the son to mark the younger Mr. Kim's 40th birthday in February.

AFP/GETTY IMAGES

Kim Il-sung (front) with his son Kim Jong-il (right) at the 6th Congress of the Workers' Party of Korea in October 1980.

Many of the celebrations, which will include gymnastics, mass singing of "hymns" in praise of the two leaders and immense banquets, will be held in newly constructed structures — one of which the intelligence sources said cost more than $50 million. The funds for the birthday celebrations were said by the intelligence officials to be coming from a special account that does not figure in North Korea's annual budget, but no estimate of the total cost was available here or in Tokyo.

In Tokyo, North Korean sources say that Kim Jong-il already runs the Government in Pyongyang for his father "on a day-to-day basis." While his father lives, Kim Jong-il is not expected to have absolute power, intelligence officials said. There will be a gradual transfer of authority "over the next five years," according to a spokesman for the Agency for National Security Planning, which was formerly known as the Korean Central Intelligence Agency.

SUPPORTERS PUT IN KEY POSTS

The rise to power of Kim Jong-il has been underscored by the promotion of his supporters, according to Kim Chang Soon, president of the Institute for North Korean Studies here. The younger Mr. Kim holds the post of first secretary of the North Korean Communist Party under his father, who is general secretary, and is ranked second in the Politburo to Oh Jin Woo, the Defense Minister.

Backers of the son who have been promoted by the father are said to include Oh Kyuk Ryul, chief of staff of the armed forces, who was a high school classmate of Kim Jong-il, and others in key army posts, to insure the backing of the 700,000-strong armed forces for Mr. Kim.

"In fact, Oh Jin Woo defers to Kim Jong-il when they appear in public," said Kim Chang Soon in an interview. "He's just a companion, a member of his retinue, so his position as No. 1 in the North Korean Politburo is nominal only."

South Korean officials said that Kim Il-sung's apparent motives in preparing the succession for his son were to guard against a sudden collapse in his reputation after he dies, as happened to Mao Zedong in China after 1976 and to Stalin after his death in 1953; to promote a successor who could not turn against him, and to maintain his control over the country even if he should become physically incapacitated.

The Kim Dynasty's North Korea: A Nation Centered on One Family

BY JOHN F. BURNS | JULY 9, 1985

WHEN THE SUMMER SUN washes over the broad boulevards and monumental buildings of this riverside capital, there is a quiet, almost deserted quality to the place, as if most of the population of 800,000 had left town for the day.

The emptiness of Pyongyang at hours when other capitals are thronged is among the most powerful impressions of North Korea, a nation that has closed its doors to much of the world since its birth at the end of World War II. The sense of being on a movie set after hours returns frequently.

In the glossy magazines and books for foreign consumption that the Government produces in prodigious quantities, the country is described as "a paradise on earth," a living monument to the genius of the man who has been in control since the Soviet Army took over from the occupation forces of Japan 40 years ago. That man is Kim Il-sung, the 73-year-old President and head of the Korean Workers' Party, who is referred to by the obligatory title of "the great leader" even by 8-year-old schoolboys.

CONTACTS ARE RESTRICTED

A weeklong visit, with official companions even for the briefest stroll and not a single opportunity for a conversation with a worker or peasant not chosen by the Government, offered little scope for penetrating the obscurities that cloak much about the country. But officially organized encounters here and in Kaesong, a city 80 miles farther south, as well as hours spent looking at the country through the windows of cars and trains, revealed the outlines of a society that imposes rigors on its citizens that are unusual even among Communist regimes.

This year, as they have done at intervals before, officials have granted visas to a handful of reporters from United States news organizations, hopeful of gaining support among Americans for a Pyongyang plan that would require the removal of United States troops from South Korea. In addition, they have been telling visitors that it is time for Americans to be disabused of what they call distortions written by reporters who previously visited here.

It seems unlikely that perceptions will change. Although officials are invariably courteous, an improvement on the brusqueness of the past, there is no sign of a diminution in the ceaseless adulation of Mr. Kim, in the exacting regimentation of daily life for the country's almost 20 million citizens, or in the aura of secrecy that cloaks even mundane things. Nor can a visitor leave without a sense that the mainspring of the society is a pervasive fear.

As North Korean officials tell it, the long hours each week that all citizens spend studying the utterances of Mr. Kim and the subordination of the individual to the group at nearly every turn are the product of an overwhelming popular enthusiasm for the leader. The enthusiasm comes, they say, from the "good things" — in housing, education, medical care — that Mr. Kim has given the people.

STRESS ON KIM'S IDEAS, NOT ON COMMUNISM

Nonetheless, visits around the country reinforce an impression of a society dedicated to one principle above all others, the glorification of a leader and the continuation of his power. Virtually the only other topic that officials are eager to discuss is reunification with the South, but even that is subsidiary to the energy spent impressing visitors with the "brilliance" of Mr. Kim and of his son and nominated successor, Kim Jong-il, 42.

In a week, no official at any level mentioned Communism. Nor was there any allusion to Marxism-Leninism, except when it was raised by a visitor. Instead, there was incessant reference to the "juche sasang," the name given to the ideology propounded by Mr. Kim. Essentially a doctrine of self-reliance, it is said to be the key to progress in every field of endeavor, more important than any scientific thesis.

Among other things, the Kim cult has effectively buried religion, at least as a public matter, although officials say pockets of Buddhism survive. In the place of the temples and churches they offer a new shrine in the lovely parkland at Mangyongdae, several miles outside the capital. Here, in a 19th-century gravedigger's cottage with mud walls and wooden beams, restored to immaculate condition, is the official birthplace of the portly, bespectacled Mr. Kim.

As visitors approach the thatched cottage at the foot of a wooded hillside, solemn organ music filters through the trees, as though a church were hidden among the pines. Along this path, in reverential groups marching behind fluttering red flags, nearly two million citizens come each year to pay obeisance to the man known as "immortal father," "genius of revolution" and dozens of equally adulatory sobriquets.

The official legend that has grown up around Mr. Kim has been extended to envelop his entire family. At Mangyongdae visitors are told that the "heroic" traditions stretch back to the leader's great-grandfather, who is said to have sunk an American "warship," the General Sherman, when it appeared in Korean waters in the 19th century. The ship was actually a trade vessel. A similar hagiography envelops Mr. Kim's father, mother and uncle.

Many of the tales of the family's accomplishments stretch credibility. In South Korea, much of the legend is described as fake. The North Korean leader's detractors have maintained at various times that he is not the original Kim Il-sung but an impostor who assumed the identity of a man who founded a guerrilla struggle against occupying Japanese forces in the 1930's. Another version says that Mr. Kim spent the key years of the struggle against the Japanese getting a political grooming in Moscow. Most of the evidence to the contrary that is offered here is in the form of paintings, not photographs.

In any case, officials insist that Mr. Kim has fashioned a political system that will outlive him. But a number of diplomats, both Western and Communist, said the size of the cult and the austere nature of life here could make him an inviting target for "de-mythification" by a future leader, much as Stalin and Mao Zedong were denounced by their successors.

EFFORT TO BUILD UP THE YOUNGER KIM

Mr. Kim's answer to this has been the advancement of his son, who has increasingly taken over important public duties, including a much-ballyhooed official visit to China in 1983. Officials deny there is a dynasty in the making, saying the choice of the "most sagacious and energetic" young man as the country's next leader was dictated by his talents. It is on him, they say, that "carrying on the revolution" depends.

Like his father, the younger Kim has an obligatory title, "the dear leader," and his own series of adulatory books. He also merits his own red plastic plaques mounted over the doorway of every room in every institution that he has visited, often mounted alongside the identical plaques for his father. Sometimes, the plaques record as many as 25 different visits. Where an object he has inspected is judged of particular significance, such as a champion ram in an agricultural museum, it gets a plaque of its own.

Outsiders looking for signs that things may change get little encouragement from the public profile of the younger Kim, who has his father's portly build and leaden way with words. A Western diplomat who wonders whether the son will be able to hold off challenges from powerful rivals of his father's generation when the transition comes says dyspeptically, "He doesn't look like a leader, he looks like a leader's son."

It is the first time that any Communist leader has tried to devolve power directly to a member of his own family. This, and the extent of the cults that have enveloped the two Kims, cause a shaking of heads even among Soviet-bloc representatives here. "It cannot be explained in rational terms," an Eastern European diplomat told a companion aboard a train outside Pyongyang. His words protected from eavesdroppers by the clattering of the carriage wheels, the diplomat added, "What is going on here has reached a stage where one must talk about the abnormal."

Toward the end of this correspondent's stay officials said that any "objective" report would acknowledge, as one of them put it, "that the reason we respect our great leader so much is that our country has a 5,000-year history in which we have suffered very much, and now, because of our great leader, we are living very well."

By closely supervising the visit from early in the morning until late at night, the officials made verification of their claims difficult. But visits to a school, a hospital, a department store and a worker's apartment, among others, as well as observations of life along the way, suggested that material standards here have risen sharply since the Korean War, to a level that many in the developing world, including China, might envy.

Nonetheless, the intensity of the praise for Mr. Kim and the unvarying formulations with which they were expressed, coupled with the apparent lack of enthusiasm among those voicing them, left the strong impression that "an undying love" for Mr. Kim and his son, as one official publication put it, is less a matter of gratitude than of compulsion. By comparison, Chinese who spoke in awed terms of Chairman Mao during the latter years of his life seemed relatively eager.

Almost the first thing a visitor sees on entering the country at Sinuiju, the border city across the Yalu River from China, is a massive alabaster statue of Mr. Kim in a heroic, striding pose. His statues dominate every city and town, his unsmiling portraits adorn most public buildings, tomes by him and about him fill bookshops to the exclusion of virtually everything else, and his sayings are emblazoned everywhere, even on granite tablets beside country roads.

ICONOGRAPHY TO RIVAL THAT OF MEDIEVAL CHURCH

The iconography is reminiscent of the imagery of the medieval Christian church. Paintings and billboards depict Kim Il-sung standing a head taller than those clustered about him, usually a step or two ahead and the subject of adoring gazes. Where he is depicted alone, or with his son, it is often in an other-worldly setting, as in a wall-sized painting in the lobby of a Pyongyang hotel that shows the two men on a mountaintop at sunset.

All photographs and paintings excise the melon-sized goiter Mr. Kim has had for at least 20 years. Although Pyongyang has hospitals with the latest Western surgical equipment, the North Korean leader is said by diplomats to have resisted attempts to remove the growth. Speculation on the reason for this usually centers less on his medical concerns than on his purported fear that political enemies might take advantage of an operation to remove him permanently.

Although invoking his name and citing his sayings is a reflex with officials, they profess to know very little about him personally. Diplomats offer little more information, saying that he is genial in his audiences with visiting dignitaries but obsessively secretive about his movements. He is a widower and is said to be a light smoker and fond of hunting. An official of the Government's Information Department said Mr. Kim lives "in a small house, just like an ordinary person," but diplomats say he has a choice of palatial residences, in the capital and elsewhere.

Writing books about him and his son is an industry, with more than 1,000 titles listed in the catalogue of the Grand People's Study House. The study house is a 600-room library overlooking Kim Il-sung Square in Pyongyang. It was built in 1982 to commemorate Mr. Kim's 70th birthday, an official holiday, as is the birthday of his son. In the simplicity of their style and content the books seem akin to children's fables, and, like them, they have a simple moral: everything of value to the nation, from the health of its children to the size of its fish catch, depends on the Kims. One recently published book on the younger Kim,

"The Great Teacher of Journalists," chronicles the "brilliant guidance" he has given to the profession, including an incident in 1980 when a reporter was "brought back to life" by his efforts. After detailing Mr. Kim's intervention — arranging an emergency flight, specifying the flight route and assembling a medical team — the book concludes that the writer's life "was indeed a new life born of the great love of our dear leader."

Virtually every economic, technical and social advance since the founding of the nation in 1945 is attributed to "on-the-spot guidance" or "instructions" issued by the two leaders. While touring the Bonghwa lock gates east of Pyongyang, part of a major flood-control project on the Daedong River, an official noted proudly that Kim Il-sung's journeys into the provinces of this New York State-sized country had taken him the equivalent of "eight times around the world," although people did not always see him because of his habit of making visits "at night."

A GIFT FOR THE OBVIOUS IN LEADERS' 'INSTRUCTIONS'

Sometimes the "guidance" appears to have been a matter of common sense, as when a guide at an agricultural science exhibition said that rice yields improved enormously after the older Mr. Kim pointed out that more seedlings could be grown if they were planted in a zigzag pattern, instead of in straight lines. Such "instructions" are presented as having come as revelations to scientists.

Although official biographies say Mr. Kim took up full-time guerrilla warfare against the occupying Japanese forces at the age of 13, he is credited with extensive technical expertise. Guides at the lock gates asserted that he and his son chose the site for the gates, checked the blueprints and gave detailed instructions to workers. The older Kim was said to have decided on the speed of the escalators in the Pyongyang subway.

Where no direct guidance is cited, officials invoke the influence of Kim Il-sung's "juche sasang," or juche idea. Its place in the national life is symbolized in a massive "tower of the juche idea," 560 feet high and topped by a "torch" of illuminated red glass, that stands beside the Daedong River in the capital. It was dedicated to Mr. Kim on his 70th birthday and is said to symbolize the "contribution to world history" made by his thought.

Children are barely old enough to read before they are required to spend hours each week "studying" the doctrine. Among Government and party officials there is a mandatory study month every year, and all other workers put in at least half a day a week reading Mr. Kim's writings or listening to readings of his speeches. When asked to define the doctrine officials become terse, saying that its essence lies in the idea that the destiny of mankind rests with the "masses."

To an outsider, there is a numbing quality in the millions of words that the Pyongyang presses have poured forth on the juche idea, also known as "Kimilsungism." The term refers to the ideology of self-reliance. A typical definition, offered in a book entitled "Comrade Kim Il-sung, an Ingenious Thinker and Theoretician," says the juche idea is "a powerful ideo-theoretical weapon with which all countries are fully able to carry their revolution and construction to victory."

"The juche idea," the book says, "is an idea of taking the attitude of a master, an independent and creative stand, toward the revolution and construction. To take the attitude of a master toward revolution and construction is a basic requirement of the juche idea. The attitude of the master finds its expression in the independent and creative stand. The independent and creative stand is essential to the establishment of juche."

The doctrine has spawned an industry of interpreters and proselytizers. North Korean money has been used to finance dozens of "juche study centers" around the world, mostly in developing countries, and the tower displays 237 marble plaques from "juche study groups" in places as far afield as New York and Caracas. Experts in the doctrine claim that it is supplanting Marxism as the ideological tool of revolutionaries around the world.

In a "question and answer" room at the Grand People's Study House, a man who identified himself as a professor of the doctrine, Pak Su Du, interrupted a counseling session with a middle-aged worker to assert that although the juche idea had "some connections" with Marxism, it had gone beyond the works of the German philosopher. "The times are different now, requiring new solutions," he said. "The theories created by our great leader accord with the realities of our present time."

Library officials nodded, evidently recognizing an answer they had heard many times before. A few doors away, in a reading room set aside for the study of Mr. Kim's writings, several hundred people identified by officials as students and off-duty workers sat in neat rows poring over the hard-backed tomes. Close to the front, cloth cap pulled down over his eyes, a man of about 30 sat with his head on a pile of books, gently snoring.

Newspapers, radios and television stations offer news only about Kim Il-sung and his son and heir apparent, Kim Jong-il, their ideology and achievements, and accounts about visitors from Communist and third-world nations. North Korean radios are designed so that listeners can tune in only to Government stations.

North Koreans usually need Government approval before they can marry, the report says, and premarital sex is harshly punished. The state supervises the rearing and education of children, whose admittance to secondary school often hinges on their class background.

Great Leader to Dear Leader

BY NICHOLAS D. KRISTOF | AUG. 20, 1989

NORTH KOREA is not so much a nation as a religion. For a skeptical foreigner to enter this normally closed country is an eerie sensation. Although Koreans are friendly and welcoming, their perception of the world is so different from ours, and their political piety so ostentatious, that reality and unreality seem to blend and blur. It is like poor science fiction, a trip to a land of antimatter where reality is the reverse of what it is at home.

Here, the reality — carefully buttressed by "evidence" in numerous museums — is that it was the United States that launched the Korean War on June 25, 1950, not the North Korean Army. Here the people fear invasion by the American imperialists, not the North Korean aggressors. Here the portly 47-year-old Kim Jong-il is not a terrorist, as he is labeled in the West, but the "Dear Leader," and a beacon for all humanity. Here, the holy trinity is not a Catholic teaching, but the substance of Korean worship: the father, "Great Leader" Kim Il-sung; the son, Dear Leader Kim Jong-il; and the holy spirit of Juche, the national ideology of self-reliance.

A Westerner visiting North Korea inevitably feels like an atheist at a convention of evangelists. The faith expressed in the Great Leader and the Dear Leader seems so excessive that it cannot possibly be genuine, and yet everyone insists that it is — even the children, girls like Han Sun Sil and Li Yong Sil. Both bright-eyed 14-year-olds, neatly dressed in blue school uniforms with red scarves that mark them as Young Pioneers, Miss Han and Miss Li were skipping down the street in the city of Nampo, hurrying toward a noodle stand to buy lunch, when they encountered something downright scary: an American. They knew about Americans — how the American imperialists forcibly occupy South Korea and terrorize the population — but they had never actually seen one until a reporter leaped out of his car to interview them.

"We call the Great Leader and Dear Leader our true fathers," Miss Han explained. "They give everything to children, and the Great Leader calls children the kings of the country. So we feel that they are our real fathers."

"The Great Leader is the ever-victorious commander who defeated two enemies in one generation," they continued, referring to Japan and the United States — only now they were speaking in unison, and behaving as if it was the most normal thing in the world for two teen-age girls to share an identical thought and spontaneously express it in one voice.

In North Korea, the entire population seems to live on a stage — people rehearse their lines so well that it is often impossible to tell when they are speaking from the heart and when from memory. From nursery school on, the regimentation and indoctrination are inescapable. In the living room of every North Korean home, near the framed photographs of the Great Leader and the Dear Leader that hang in virtually every room in the country, a small box juts out from the wall. These loudspeakers might be seen as umbilical cords linking North Koreans to their mother-Government, by piping propaganda into every home. Even when peasants are working in the fields, they are bombarded with propaganda from outdoor speakers.

Just in case anyone should miss the point of all this propaganda, the authorities have named one suburb of Pyongyang, the capital city — Paradise.

Probably no society is so tightly monitored and controlled in all the world, and anyone who expresses "mental illness," as one Korean official described dissent, is promptly banished from the capital with his entire family. Any dissident would have to be breathtakingly brave, or stunningly foolish; disloyalty threatens not only one's own future, but that of the entire family. Entrance into university, admission to the party, access to jobs and housing — all these depend on loyalty. As a foreign resident of Pyongyang put it, "If in England people are classified by accent, and in America by their wealth, here they are classified by their loyalty to the Kims."

The North Koreans' avowals of faith in the Great Leader and the Dear Leader are so worshipful that Westerners tend to think that they protest too much, that the faith must be forced. But it may be that in the majority of cases people really do love the Great Leader and the Dear Leader.

Perhaps the best metaphor for North Korea is the medieval church. Much of the population consists of genuine believers, and no one pays enormous attention to the minority of heretics who are tortured and killed, the way witches or Christians of a dissident sect were killed during the Middle Ages. The state devotes vast resources to unproductive but stylish investments — such as the enormous army and the countless grand monuments to the Great Leader — just as medieval England and France spent lavishly on the crusades and on soaring cathedrals to glorify God. Maybe some ordinary North Koreans think in their hearts that it is a waste for Pyongyang to build marble-lined subway stations, but a good many probably accept it with piety or resignation, just as penniless congregations accepted the grand construction projects of old.

This country of some 21 million might be regarded merely as a peculiarity, a laboratory drawn from Orwell's imagination, were it not for the very real threat of armed conflict. The demilitarized zone that divides the country from the vigorous capitalist South remains a bitterly contested area of conflicting visions and ambitions. And though representatives of each side hold periodic meetings in a small one-room building that straddles the border at Panmunjom, there is no real dialogue; the two sides talk at each other. There is little sign that peace is likely to break out soon.

North Korea fields the world's fifth-largest military force, including an estimated 840,000 troops; but the menace of the country might be better symbolized by a few large buildings on a road near the city of Yongbyon, north of Pyongyang. Though the road is normally closed to foreigners (foreigners are usually allowed to travel only on specially-identified roads, and even then mainly at night), satellite photographs make it clear that one of these buildings is a small nuclear reactor. Beside the reactor is a building that Western intelligence experts believe is a reprocessing center — to convert nuclear waste into material that could be used for a nuclear bomb.

At least two Asians, one of whom regularly visits the country, have seen the facility, as they were driven by on the way to somewhere else, in what apparently was a rare lapse by the security apparatus. In an interview last month, they said that what they saw almost surely was a nuclear reactor. An official with some access to North Korean Government leaders said in an interview around the same time that the adjacent building was indeed a reprocessing center, adding that it had been built with Soviet technology. If correct, this confirms the fears of South Korean and Western intelligence officers that North Korea may be developing the capacity to build a nuclear bomb.

The fear of North Korea as a potential flashpoint is heightened by the transition now under way, from the Great Leader — 77-year-old Kim Il-sung — to the Dear Leader — his 47-year-old son, Kim Jong-il. Many foreign analysts believe Kim Jong-il has been associated with a string of terrorist incidents, among them the 1983 bomb attack in Rangoon that wiped out a large part of the South Korean Cabinet and the 1987 bombing of a civilian South Korean airliner. And because Kim Jong-il lacks his father's charisma and heroic past, there are fears that Kim Jong-il will try to prove his "heroic" credentials by engaging in some aggressive action against his enemies.

Kim Jong-il is rapidly gaining control of day-to-day decision making. "During the last five months, the changeover has become more visible," said a foreigner living in Pyongyang. "Whether he will last is anybody's guess, but the transition will be smooth. It has been systematized down to the last bolt."

The Dear Leader must maintain his family's imperial and totalitarian control while somehow confronting North Korea's deepening economic problems. His burdens include a stagnating economy that barely managed 3 percent annual growth during the last decade, at a time when the country's rival to the south averaged 9 percent and North Korea's traditional backers in the Communist bloc are showing increasing enthusiasm for doing business with Seoul.

This economic and diplomatic malaise — and the perception that the country is being left behind — could yet inspire North Korea to lurch toward more pragmatic policies — or into new dangers and confrontations.

From abroad, North Korea is generally viewed as an impoverished land whose people are terrified of foreigners and of one another, a nation as devoid of human spontaneity as of foreign exchange. The reality is more complicated. Pyongyang, for example, is a beautiful, well-planned capital in a continent where capitals tend to be polluted and crowded. Impressive construction projects are everywhere: enormous museums, an Arch of Triumph bigger than the one in Paris, and the ubiquitous, elegant statues of Kim Il-sung. Some factories are modern and boast imported high-technology equipment. North Korea has defaulted on its $5 billion foreign debt, but not because it has no foreign exchange — it simply could not resist the temptation to spend the money on its own purposes.

The Pyongyang No. 1 High School boasts a Japanese scanning microscope that can magnify 70,000 times, as well as computer classes in which there is a Japanese-made personal computer and printer for each student. The language labs are more modern than those in American high schools, letting even junior high school students master their textbook's description, in English, of New York City: "A city of huge skyscrapers, yes — but not far from them you will find lots of houses with three or four floors only … Over a million New Yorkers have to live in miserable flats."

It is clear these are Potemkin schools and Potemkin factories; indeed, the entire nation is geared to impress foreigners. But though one's initial impression is that everything is a facade behind which must lie a grim life of poverty, this does not seem quite accurate. One foreigner in Pyongyang who has traveled in the countryside reported that rural clinics lack incubators and other equipment; but he also noted that in most of Asia the villages are much poorer than the cities.

In North Korea, however, villagers are not allowed to move to the city to improve their lot. And in its fervor to make Pyongyang a beautiful, orderly city, the Government appears to have moved out all the handicapped and mentally retarded people. Nobody rides a bicycle in the center of the city, apparently because the Government frowns on them; they are regarded as old-fashioned and unnecessary now that Pyongyang has a subway that is one of the most beautiful in the world. Its trains rush along every few minutes, and the marble-lined stations are spotless; there is, needless to say, no graffiti.

North Korean officials maintain there has never been a rape or murder in the country. Li Chol Sin, the official in charge of cultural relations with the West, concedes that very occasionally there are thefts, mainly by "young pranksters," but he contends that North Korea has no prisons. Instead, he said, there are "re-education centers" for those who have made mistakes, such as drivers who run down pedestrians.

"You foreigners will never understand Korea," officials say again and again. And perhaps they are right — quasi-religious feelings for a political leader seem incomprehensible to most Americans. But a Chinese who lived for many years in North Korea said that the reverence for the Kim family reminded him of the emotions many Chinese once felt for Chairman Mao Zedong. It was a cult of personality, and unmerited, the Chinese said, but at one time it was overwhelmingly sincere. He noted that life in North Korea had improved over the years, but not quite so quickly as in South Korea, China or some other countries. Ordinary North Koreans do not know this; information is so strictly regulated that they believe their country is an oasis of wealth and stability in a cruel and impoverished world. North Koreans who study at Beijing University, for example, often must go through a difficult adjustment. Having been told that China is very backward, and having seen 30-year-old Chinese movies that seem to support this, they then arrive in Beijing to discover that many people eat and dress better than they do.

Even the defectors who harshly criticize North Korea in a long and carefully researched report published last December by the human rights group Asia Watch acknowledge that North Koreans generally are not critical of their leaders.

"I never felt that my human rights were oppressed," one defector says in the report. "Nor did I realize that there were other kinds of ways to live in other parts of the world. People ... were so indoctrinated and organized into a rigidly closed society that they did not know anything else. In that regard, there was no unhappiness from any sense of human rights oppression."

Perhaps because I am based in China, I found the relatively relaxed atmosphere particularly surprising. I expected North Korea, like China after the June 4 crackdown, to be a society in which people were afraid to talk to foreigners and the Government was afraid to allow foreign reporters to interview ordinary Koreans.

In fact, there was little of the cloud of fear that hangs over China these days, and the Korean authorities were willing to let ordinary people be interviewed. Eventually, I understood the difference: In China, the Government knows that if ordinary citizens are allowed to speak to foreigners they will likely launch into scathing attacks on the authorities. In North Korea, the Government knows that most people will gush praise for the Great Leader. The North Koreans are better trained, or better brainwashed, or more fearful, or more devout — whatever it is, from the Government's point of view they are more reliable.

For most of its history, North Korea has been tightly sealed. The only foreign journalists stationed in Pyongyang are Chinese and Russian; the Westerners living in the country could fit around a dinner table. This dinner party would include a single Finnish diplomat with his wife, a Swedish United Nations official, a few French and West German engineers and businessmen, several young Englishmen and others who come to help polish Government translations into their languages, and a lone and mysterious American who defected many years ago.

At one time, the dinner table might also have included a coterie of young Swedish women who were brought in by the Government for purposes better left to the imagination. Reportedly, they sometimes danced, without much clothing, at Kim Jong-il's parties, and there are wilder rumors about private liaisons. It's not clear if any Swedish women remain in Pyongyang, but for the last two years at least the diplomatic party given for Kim Jong-il's birthday has not included any — though there have been virtually topless Korean dancers, an astonishing anomaly in a nation that preaches revolutionary virtue. Kim Jong-il does not attend these diplomatic parties himself, but closed-circuit television cameras can be seen scanning the scene, and East Bloc diplomats say that the Dear Leader watches from another room.

The Dear Leader is the scion of a family dynasty that has been linked to North Korea's history since before the nation's founding. During the 1930's, Kim Il-sung was the leader of a small band of revolutionary nationalists fighting the Japanese occupation. After the Japanese defeat, the Soviet Union supported Kim Il-sung as leader of the northern half of the peninsula, and he consolidated his control by eliminating all opposition. Mr. Kim established a Stalinist economic system emphasizing heavy industry and mass mobilization; private enterprise was banned, and the emphasis put on Juche, self-reliance. In fact, by international standards North Korea's economic performance has been fairly impressive until recently, but the country has the misfortune to be situated next to one of the 20th century's miracle economies, and inevitably it is humiliated by the comparison.

During the early 1970's, it became obvious that President Kim had settled on a system of succession that was more imperial than Communist — passing on control of the nation to his eldest son. A new legend had to be born.

Kim Jong-il was born on Feb. 16, 1942, apparently in the Soviet Union. But it is not fitting for a nationalist hero to be born in the Soviet Union, and so it was ordained that Kim Jong-il was born in a secret camp of anti-Japanese guerrillas on Mount Paekdu, in the mountainous north of the peninsula. The spot, which has been turned into a shrine, could not have been more appropriate for a Korean leader; Mount Paekdu is a sacred mountain revered by both North and South Koreans as the place where the mythic progenitor Tangun founded the nation 5,000 years ago. Kim Jong-il, in short, emerges as a modern incarnation of Tangun. Indeed, an official history has the infant "raising a cry at his birth, as if it were a signal for the attainment of the Korean people's aspirations."

After graduation from Kim Il-sung University in 1963, Kim Jong-il began working in the headquarters of the Korean Workers' Party, the local equivalent of the Communist Party. Like 5,000 other party officials, he worked — and still works — in a pleasant-looking neighborhood in the center of Pyongyang. It is pleasant-looking, that is, until you try to enter, and are suddenly confronted by guards with submachine guns who turn you away.

Hailed as the "sole successor" and No. 2 in the country in 1980, Kim Jong-il launched his own personality cult, and one possible source of rivalry, his stepmother, was sharply demoted. Soon almost all top officials were either of Kim Il-sung's generation or Kim Jong-il's.

Because Kim Jong-il has never been given a major job to test him, it is difficult to know what his policies would be. "It is to his advantage not to have a particular position," explained a foreign resident of Pyongyang. "If anything goes wrong, he's not there. But if everything goes right, then it's under the guidance of the Dear Leader."

Kim Jong-il is said to be a great film buff, with an underground library of thousands of foreign movies, and he seems to have nurtured North Korea's own burgeoning film industry. The purpose of the films, which are shown in theaters throughout the country, is not so much to entertain as to cultivate proper political attitudes. The vast Korean Feature Film Studio, not far from Pyongyang, is extremely impressive — though one can't help wondering whether it makes sense for a nation that cannot pay its foreign debt to create such an enormous film studio. Kim Jong-il has visited the studio 320 times since 1963 — the studio officials keep careful count — and has often made suggestions for how movies should be edited to maximize their impact.

Lee Sok Kyu, a liaison official at the studio who said he had met the Dear Leader on one visit, exuded praise for his esthetic judgment and compassion. "I was ill at the time," Mr. Lee said, "and so later he sent me some deer blood as a tonic. It was very helpful."

Not everyone in the film industry is so enthusiastic, particularly the couple Choi Un Hui and Shin Sang Ok. Miss Choi was a famous South Korean actress and Mr. Shin, her husband, a well-known director when they took a trip to Hong Kong in 1978 — where, they say, they were kidnapped and brought to North Korea on orders of Kim Jong-il, who wanted to improve North Korean movies. In 1986, they say, after convincing Kim Jong-il that they believed in him and could be trusted, they escaped while on a trip to Vienna. (North Korean officials claim Miss Chou and Mr. Shin voluntarily defected to North Korea, then absconded with large amounts of money.) The couple published a two-volume account of their experience in North Korea. By their account, Kim Jong-il is a bold and impulsive man, inclined to reach for the phone at any hour to resolve a problem.

North Korea is generally held responsible for two spectacular terrorist attacks: the 1983 bombing of a shrine in Rangoon, Burma, that killed at least 19 people, including seven high-ranking South Korean officials; and the 1987 midair bombing of a South Korean airliner, which killed 115 people. The two terrorists who left the time bomb on the plane were captured, and one survived a joint suicide attempt and was interrogated and tried in Seoul. She identified herself as Kim Ilyon Hui, the 26-year-old daughter of a career diplomat from Pyongyang, and said she had been given instructions that were said to originate with Kim Jong-il. She said that before leaving for the mission she took an oath before a portrait of Kim Jong-il: "I will fight to the death for the lofty authority and prestige of the Dear Leader." She was sentenced to death, but it is widely expected that this will be commuted.

Kim Jong-il now seems set to inherit North Korea on his father's death, but some analysts doubt he will last very long. "The father really is very charismatic," said a diplomat who frequently visits North Korea. "The son is pudgy, short and ugly. He's a young, spoiled upstart. He wants toys, women, films — he's got them. And he's always been in the shadow of his father, so he's stunted. After the succession, the whole place will unravel."

Kim Il-sung, it is said, looks like a leader, Kim Jong-il like a leader's son. Those who doubt Kim Jong-il will last predict that after the father dies, resistance will emerge from the "old revolutionaries" of the father's generation and force the son out of power. Much will depend on the loyalty of the military. In recent years, military leaders have often been shuffled, and there have been occasional rumors about assassination plots against Kim Il-sung or Kim Jong-il, but nothing can be confirmed.

Still, some analysts maintain that Kim Jong-il has already cemented his position and can survive indefinitely in a system in which dissent is ruthlessly suppressed and all those with power have risen because of their associations with the Kim family. North Korea, after all, is totalitarian in the most fundamental sense: the Government controls the totality of life. People wake up in the morning when the speaker on their wall squawks to life, go to their Government-assigned jobs, then study political thought — which means, largely, the thought of the Kims.

This sounds sinister; but though one expects the country to be gray and menacing, it isn't. North Koreans laugh and enjoy themselves, tease one another and tell dirty jokes, flirt and hold hands. And when they talk about their Great Leader or, now, their Dear Leader, they smile and smile.

For the Great Leader at 80, a Great Birthday Bash

BY DAVID E. SANGER | MAY 11, 1992

THESE HAVE BEEN a busy few weeks in Paradise.

Every day for weeks now, thousands of North Koreans have poured into the national stadium here to watch the "mass games" in honor of the 80th birthday of Kim Il-sung, the country's perpetually lauded "Great Leader." With endless waves of students streaming onto the field in regimented rows, this is not your ordinary half-time show. Teaching came to a halt in many Pyongyang schools months ago so that 100,000 children could practice for the daily gymnastic extravaganza, learning the somersaults and synchronized wrist flips needed to create an ever-changing tableau of the Great Leader with thousands of hand-held placards.

For North Koreans whose tastes lean toward higher culture, there is always the opera, "My Happy Country With a Great Leader." It plays nightly to a packed house. And in the Reunification Housing Project across town, workers are furiously preparing 50,000 apartments that are one of the Great Leader's birthday gifts to his people. Never mind that heat and electricity are in short supply, keeping many from moving in.

With North Korea's economy in a shambles, its oil supplies from Russia dwindling, meat hard to find and former Communist allies finding friends elsewhere, one might think that festivities for the only leader this country has ever known might be a bit muted. Quite to the contrary. Mr. Kim has been granted the title of "Generalissimo" — perhaps the only title he lacked until now — and signs have been put up everywhere urging the people to study his teachings anew.

"The worse things get, the louder everyone becomes about the Great Leader's infallibility," an Eastern European diplomat here said the other day. "This place just gets scarier and scarier."

FESTIVITIES COSTING MILLIONS

By the most conservative estimates, the celebrations in honor of Mr. Kim — and the 50th birthday of his son, Kim Jong-il, the "Dear Leader" and heir apparent — cost this country tens of millions of dollars. But North Korea's leaders reject any suggestions that the money might be better spent overhauling the nearly moribund economy, or feeding people in regions where there are fears of malnutrition.

"Of course the economy is facing some hardships," Kim Dal Hyon, the deputy prime minister, told a group of visiting foreign correspondents recently. "And it costs a bit of money to construct all these new memorials. But we have to pay it. We have to educate our people. Because of this, we don't have any social evils like alcohol, drugs and so forth."

One of North Korea's few admitted evils, however, is sloppy bookkeeping. Mr. Kim said he simply could not estimate how much the celebrations cost. "You know," he added, "the main shortcoming of all socialist countries is that we are not clever with figures."

GERHARD JOREN/LIGHTROCKET/GETTY IMAGES

A celebration for Kim Il-sung's 80th birthday at Kim Il-sung Stadium in Pyongyang.

For North Korea-watchers, the past few weeks have been full of little surprises, the kind that in another era would have tickled Kremlinologists. For example, for the first time North Koreans heard the voice of Kim Jong-il, who heads one of the world's largest armies but whose public utterances had never before been broadcast. Granted it was not much — "Glory to the heroic Korean People's Army!" he shouted at the end of a goose-stepping parade by the 1.1 million-member military — but it was played over and over on the nightly rebroadcasts of the festivities. Parade highlights are also being played daily on the radio.

'WE ENVY NOBODY'

For the people, the celebrations have clearly been a boon. China sent several hundred thousand tons of pork, and the Government distributed coupons to supplement the monthly allotment of 4.4 pounds of meat and chicken for every person. For the Government, the celebrations have been turned into a chance to declare, once again, that North Korea is different, and that the principles of self-sufficiency have enabled it to escape the pitfalls that brought down less foresighted Communist regimes.

In between displays of karate skills and wild acrobatics at the stadium, the thousands holding placards flash the message that the Government says it is trying to send around the world this spring. "We Envy Nobody in the World!" declares one. "Let's Have Our Own Style Socialism!" implores another. And, for any who wondered, there was one more proclamation, "We Are Happy!"

Such messages are also explicit in North Korea's newest bestseller, Kim Il-sung's memoirs of his years fighting the Japanese occupation. The book came out two weeks ago, but it is already a key part of the curriculum at Pyongyang High Middle School No. 1, a sparkling, well-equipped institution that visitors to the city are guided through as an example of the country's educational system. In one classroom on a recent Saturday morning, a teacher was reading chapters from the memoirs to his students. They sat stiffly in their school uniforms, eyes straight forward. No one bothered taking notes.

Upstairs, in the physics laboratory, Li Chun Ran, a lively 17-year-old with a quick smile, proudly showed off what she received during the celebrations: a fresh, blue school uniform. "Kim Il-sung and the Dear Leader, Kim Jong-il, gave me the dress," she said, adding that the gift had doubled her resolve to study harder. But it is a heavily-edited curriculum. Asked the nationality of the first man to land on the moon, the science students sat and pondered for a minute.

U.S. EFFORTS OVERLOOKED

"It was Russian people, I think," one finally volunteered. And no one recalled reading that the United States and other allies also fought for Korea's independence from Japan.

There are similar renditions of history at the opera, the story of Kim Il-sung's fight for freedom, set to classical music. There are images of the Great Leader battling the Japanese, images of him offering "guidance" about where to place petrochemical factories and how to build giant dams. There are old movie clips of an American bomber crashing during the Korean War, and the crew surrendering, prompting the audience to clap wildly. There is a cast of 5,000. And there is singing, lots of it.

Generalissimo, Kim Il-sung,
Our fatherly leader!
The people are unfailingly loyal to you!
Our party is the best in the world!
Socialism is the best in the world!
Let's defend Socialism,
Under the unfurled red banner!

Kim Il-sung, Enigmatic 'Great Leader' of North Korea for 5 Decades, Dies at 82

BY DAVID E. SANGER | JULY 10, 1994

BY THE TIME Kim Il-sung died on Friday at the age of 82, there was not one "Great Leader" running North Korea. There were three.

There was the man seen around the world as a Stalinist maniac, who 44 years ago sent his troops pouring over the 38th parallel to unify the Korean Peninsula on his own terms, and who four decades later burst again onto the front pages as a man in search of a nuclear bomb to save his regime. This was the Kim who intimidated his neighbors into silence, who used his unpredictability as a weapon.

There was the Kim Il-sung of North Korean myth, whose likeness dominates Pyongyang and every town square in the form of 30,000 statues, the man who was lionized in song as the "sun of the country" for single-handedly defeating two enemies in one generation: Japan and the United States.

And, in recent years, there was the grandfatherly Kim Il-sung, the smiling leader seeking respect for his economically disabled nation, the man who three weeks ago embraced Jimmy Carter and used him as a conduit to President Clinton, who was not yet born when Mr. Kim was installed as North Korea's leader. It was that incarnation of Mr. Kim that led the former President to declare, with little hint of skepticism, that a "miracle" had occurred. One of the world's most fearsome dictators actually sounded reasonable and eager to end his confrontation with the West.

They were all images that Mr. Kim, the peasants' son who went on to become the longest-surviving Communist leader of the cold war, knew how to exploit brilliantly. When his death came early Friday morning, he had been staging a remarkable international comeback, a shadow from the old newsreels of the Korean War who thrust himself into the atomic glare of the 1990's.

AN ENDURING PUZZLE TO THE OUTSIDE WORLD

For those who met him, he was the incongruous dictator of a hard and unforgiving land. Former Representative Stephen J. Solarz of Brooklyn, who met Mr. Kim twice, said a few days ago:

> *He has this avuncular persona that stands in stark contrast to the reality of the regime, which is without question the most ruthless and tyrannical anywhere in the world. It is like meeting Hitler at Berchtesgaden and commenting on how he got along with the dogs and the children. He has the blood of millions on his hands; he has a society based on Orwell's "1984."*
>
> *So you expect someone who will act like Saddam Hussein, a forbidding, threatening presence. And he is just the opposite, always smiling, always speaking softly.*

In fact, to step into Kim Il-sung's North Korea was to enter a laboratory from Orwell's wildest imaginings: a country that could not afford to keep the lights on at night, and yet which built — but may never open — Asia's tallest hotel, a country where the people seemed almost robotic in their praise of their leader and his son, Kim Jong-il, his presumed successor.

Millions of North Koreans, until this morning's news, have never lived in a country not run by Kim Il-sung.

During his rule North Koreans were urged to devote at least two hours a day, and four on Saturdays, to "Kim study," memorizing his sayings. His birthday was, for decades, the nation's greatest holiday, celebrated with "mass games" in which North Korean youth performed remarkable gymnastic feats.

It is a country of operas like "My Happy Country with a Great Leader," whose lyrics include:

> *O, Generalissimo, Kim Il-sung,*
> *Our fatherly leader!*

The people are unfailingly loyal to you!
Our party is the best in the world!
Socialism is the best in the world!
Let's defend Socialism,
Under the unfurled red banner!

Mr. Kim seemed, in every public utterance, to be nothing short of a god. Everything North Koreans received from the government — clothes, rice, apartments — were said to come directly from "the Great Leader" or "the Dear Leader," his son. Pyongyang considered 50,000 new apartments to be the Great Leader's birthday gifts to his people. But when a reporter toured these "gifts," no one discussed the fact that there was little heat and electricity.

"You have to remember that at home, President Kim Il-sung is treated as a combination of George Washington, Thomas Jefferson and Abe Lincoln," Mr. Carter said this week in Tokyo.

Mr. Kim's philosophy centered on the principle he called "juche," which he said meant "holding fast to the principle of solving for one-self all the problems of the revolution and construction of one's own efforts." This was to be accomplished, he added, while "applying the universal truth of Marxism-Leninism."

He held every important post in the country, including General Secretary of the Central Committee of the Workers' Party of Korea, its one party, and President of the country. And when he died, no one had yet really figured out his game: whether he was using the threat of an atomic weapon to get economic aid for his bankrupt country, or whether he was wielding it as a suicide pill to save his regime from absorption by the South.

"It is possible," one American official who has met Mr. Kim, said today, "that we will now never know."

FROM HUMBLE ORIGINS, A STEEP CLIMB TO POWER

Kim Il-sung was born to a peasant couple in a small, mud-walled house on the outskirts of Pyongyang on April 15, 1912, shortly after the Japanese began their formal occupation of Korea. For years that house has been visited daily by thousands of North Koreans.

Mr. Kim often used his simple birthplace to contrast his own early life with Pyongyang's American missionaries and Japanese residents. "In the 'Westerners village,' at the time inhabited by Americans and the Japanese settlers, brick houses, shops and churches increased in number," he recalled vividly many decades later, but across town "the slum quarters were getting bigger."

It is nearly impossible to separate truth and fiction in the state-sponsored mythology about Kim Il-sung's youth, but in all the stories there is a constant subtext: Mr. Kim's struggles against greater powers around him, particularly America and Japan.

Those two countries controlled the world in Mr. Kim's view, and it was the Kim family's destiny to battle them. In his memoirs, published two years ago, Mr. Kim maintained that his great-grandfather set fire to the General Sherman, a "U.S. imperialist aggressors' ship" because its crew went about "stealing the people's possessions and raping the women" while sailing up the Taedong River to Pyongyang in 1866. Mr. Kim's biographer at the University of Hawaii, Suh Dae Sook, calls these stories "politically motivated fabrications," but most of them seem impossible to verify or disprove.

Whether the stories are true or not, the myths have become the man.

Mr. Kim said he was a schoolchild when he committed his first act of rebellion against the Japanese occupiers, using a pocket knife to scratch off the title "Mother Tongue Reader" from the textbook issued by the Japanese colonial government, which required children to speak only Japanese. He said he wrote "Japanese Reader" on the cover, and from that moment, "whenever I saw children trying to learn Japanese, I told them Koreans must speak Korean."

Neither his memoirs nor official biographies dwell on the fact that he spent most of his youth in Manchuria, where he learned Chinese. That later turned out to be a crucial skill, as he joined China's communist guerrillas. And it was from China that Kim obtained the Communist philosophy that he combined with the nationalist mission his father bequeathed him — along with two pistols — on his deathbed in 1926: to free the peninsula from Japanese domination.

IMAGES OF RESISTANCE, MASTERFULLY MANIPULATED

Mr. Kim served as an anti-Japanese guerrilla in Manchuria, Siberia and the North Korean border areas, but it is impossible to verify the claims of his astounding feats, including the killing of a unit of Japanese special police who were tracking him in 1940. The next year, he was forced to retreat to the Soviet Union for the remainder of the war. He makes no mention of that time, perhaps because it would be too obvious that his son, the "Dear Leader," was born there in February 1942, instead of on Korea's own soil. Mr. Kim was married to Kim Chong Suk, who died in 1949.

When he reappeared in Korea in late 1945, after the Soviet Union was already administering the area, it was in the uniform of a Soviet major. It was a ticket back home: At the war's end, the country was cut roughly in half at the 38th parallel, with the Soviet Union assuming the temporary occupation of the northern part and the United States the occupation of the southern zone. Reunification of the nation was the Allies' announced goal. Quickly, and with Stalin's apparent backing, he took control of the Korean Workers Party and called for a reunification under Communist control.

Of course, Mr. Kim's emergence was far more complicated than the official accounts suggest. When he returned to Korea after 20 years' absence, his Communist party was tiny, outnumbered by other nationalist groups. But he rose to power by denouncing the "lackeys" of the Japanese and the Americans, and wiped out many of his enemies — 60,000 people in his first purge.

The Democratic People's Republic of Korea was created in September 1948 after the United States organized the first government in the South, the Republic of Korea.

When Mr. Kim led an invading army into the South in June 1950 — a scene of carnage that today seems a world away from modern Seoul — the Truman Administration saw the takeover as the first step in a far broader Communist plot, directed from Moscow and Beijing, to seize much of Asia.

But a remarkable new study published earlier this year by Stanford University Press, one that is fairly chilling read in the context of the current nuclear standoff, shows that it was Kim Il-sung who did all the plotting. Documents recently made available in Russia, along with others that have slipped out of China, indicate that Mr. Kim was convinced he could take the South in three days.

His forces met little resistance in the first weeks, and by early September had driven the South Korean Army and its American allies to the Pusan area, at the southeastern tip of the Korean peninsula.

After a brilliant beginning, Mr. Kim's war plans went astray. He was surprised when, five days after his soldiers began streaming across the 38th parallel, President Harry S. Truman authorized American land, sea and air forces to go to South Korea's aid. Eventually 15 other nations responded to the United Nations call for help. Led by Gen. Douglas MacArthur, they reacted with a counteroffensive on Sept. 15, staging a large-scale invasion at Inchon, a conquered South Korean port on the west coast about 20 miles from Seoul. MacArthur's forces pursued them back over the parallel and, on Oct. 19, captured Pyongyang. By late November Mr. Kim and his troops had been driven almost to the Yalu River on the Chinese border.

But he was a wily strategist, and with "volunteers" from the Chinese Army and Air Force and some from the Soviet Union he recaptured Seoul in January 1951 and held it briefly. For the rest of the war bitter fighting was centered nearby and roughly along the 38th parallel.

MacArthur, who wanted to carry out another invasion of North Korea, advance beyond the Yalu into China and mount a full-scale assault on Communism, was relieved of his command by Truman.

But every time there was talk of finally taking action regarding North Korea's nuclear development, the Asian allies fretted that Mr. Kim should not be provoked. The warning lights became impossible to ignore in March 1993, when the North announced it would pull out of the Nuclear Nonproliferation Treaty rather than face continued pressure for disclosure and inspections. Their withdrawal was later suspended, but inspectors were kept out.

When North Korea began removing more fuel from its reactor this spring, potentially creating material for five more nuclear weapons, the United States moved for United Nations sanctions.

As fears of a confrontation grew, the United States sent more equipment to its bases in Japan and South Korea, from Patriot missiles to ammunition to laser-guided bombs.

In the last weeks of his life, Mr. Kim had one brilliant maneuver left. He let Mr. Carter, who was deeply opposed to sanctions, take up a two-year-old invitation to come visit Pyongyang as a private citizen. After the first night of talks, Mr. Carter went on television to announce that the Great Leader was ready to deal: He would freeze the country's nuclear program while the United States talked about a range of diplomatic and economic benefits that might end the North's isolation from the world. Meanwhile, international inspectors, who had been barred from parts of the nuclear sites, could stay there. The Clinton Administration was suspicious, but eventually dove through the opening. Mr. Carter also emerged with an invitation from the South: a summit meeting between the Presidents of North and South Korea, a first since the peninsula was divided in 1945. Five decades after Asia's war ended in a precarious stalemate, it would have been a symbolic melting of the last Cold War division. For many Koreans it would have undoubtedly raised a surge of nationalism that Kim Il-sung would have applauded: Differences aside, we are all Koreans, our country divided only because we were pawns of the Cold War. He died 17 days before the meeting was to begin.

Death Doesn't End Rule of Kim Il-sung, 'Eternal President'

BY NICHOLAS D. KRISTOF | SEPT. 7, 1998

NORTH KOREA announced today that it had revised its Constitution to make its late "Great Leader," Kim Il-sung, the country's "eternal President."

Adjusting to the inconvenience of having a President who died four years ago and is thus unable to make speeches, the Supreme People's Assembly listened soberly to a tape recording of an address by President Kim delivered in 1990.

The upshot of the announcement is that, as expected, President Kim's son Kim Jong-il — the country's longtime "Dear Leader" — will in effect be head of state, based on his position as chairman of the National Defense Commission. It is not clear how much it will matter that North Korea does not have a living President, for it has already gotten by with a vacant presidency in the four years since Kim Il-sung died.

There is no doubt that Kim Jong-il controls North Korea firmly and that he could have had the presidency if he had wanted it. But scholars cite two reasons why he may have preferred to let his late father retain the post.

The first is simply to show respect and filial piety to the man who founded North Korea half a century ago and ruled it virtually as a god ever since. Though he was often condemned as a dictator in the West, Kim Il-sung seems to have been revered by many North Koreans, as even defectors usually acknowledge.

"Kim Jong-il needs his father, needs to wear his father's jacket," said Han S. Park, a scholar of North Korea at the University of Georgia. Mr. Park said that in time Kim Jong-il may gradually emerge and rule more openly on his own.

The second reason Mr. Kim may have been reluctant to take on the presidency is that it would make him a far more public figure and would oblige him to meet ambassadors and foreign visitors. He has always been an intensely private figure, a man who virtually never travels or meets foreign visitors.

Under the new Constitution, the tasks of receiving ambassadors and representing the state for diplomatic purposes will be taken over by the president of the presidium of the Supreme People's Assembly, the legislature. The president of that presidium will be Kim Yong Nam, the previous Foreign Minister.

Kim Yong Nam, who is not related to Kim Jong-il, is now ranked No. 2 in North Korea's hierarchy.

It is not clear why Kim Jong-il is so reluctant to meet foreigners and appear in public. But a top North Korean official who defected to the South, Hwang Jang Yop, has said Mr. Kim believes that he derives some charisma or power from the air of mystery that surrounds him.

North Koreans are expected to continue to focus their cult of personality on the father, whose face continues to adorn the badges worn by nearly every adult North Korean. But the son is also now referred to as "Great Leader" — although the Korean phrase used for the son is different from the one reserved for the father — and the North Korean authorities are hailing his rise to head of state as a major national triumph.

The official Korean Central News Agency today called it "a historic event and great jubilee of the nation which gives a definite guarantee for certain victory in the revolutionary struggle of the Korean people."

South Korea, for its part, urged Mr. Kim to be "responsible" and to stop building up his country's armed forces at a time when many North Koreans are starving.

CHAPTER 4

Kim Jong-il Takes Power

After the official state mourning period following Kim Il-sung's death in 1994, Kim Jong-il was declared the country's Great Leader in 1997. Foreign journalists began the complicated task of piecing together biographical details of the new leader, sifting through myths propagated by the North Korean government and popular rumors to gain a better sense of who exactly Kim Jong-il was. Depictions of the leader varied from film fanatic and playboy to a sinister and antagonistic dictator.

North Korea's Heir Apparent Meets Foreign Diplomats

BY ANDREW POLLACK | JULY 12, 1994

IN YET ANOTHER SIGN that he will become the new leader of North Korea, Kim Jong-il suddenly came out of seclusion tonight and met with foreigners for the first time since the death of his father, Kim Il-sung, on Friday.

Ambassadors stationed in North Korea's capital of Pyongyang were invited on short notice tonight to the presidential palace to see the body of Kim Il-sung and pay respects to his survivors.

The reclusive and mysterious Kim Jong-il was at the head of the receiving line, according to one diplomat who was there.

"There is no doubt that he is now the new leader of North Korea," said this diplomat, who is from Eastern Europe but insisted that he and his country not be identified.

A DISPLAY OF OPENNESS

Mr. Kim almost never meets with foreign dignitaries. But as head of state he will have to receive ambassadors and other foreigners, which is why tonight's session might be significant, this diplomat said. North Korea also released film footage of what appeared to be a diplomatic reception and other scenes of mourning, a highly symbolic display of openness in one of the world's most isolated societies.

The footage was broadcast on Japanese and South Korean television and showed Kim Il-sung lying in state in a glass coffin, while an array of weeping mourners, including his son, filed past.

The sudden appearance of the 52-year-old heir apparent before the diplomats capped a day in which North Korea began to return to normal after a frenzy of mourning over the weekend for its 82-year-old "Great Leader," who had ruled the Communist nation for nearly half a century until he died, apparently of a heart attack.

Four diplomats stationed in Pyongyang, reached by telephone today, said the city remained peaceful and was functioning normally, with no extra police officers or soldiers in evidence. The airport, train station, shops and schools were open, they said.

"Everything is absolutely calm," said an official at the embassy of an Asian country. With North Korea closed to most foreign news organizations, diplomats provided some of the few first-hand reports of what was happening there.

Thousands upon thousands of people today continued to stream toward a huge statue of the late Mr. Kim in central Pyongyang, where they cried and prostrated themselves and placed flowers.

"It more or less seems like the day that Stalin died," said one East European diplomat, referring to the mobs that thronged Moscow after Stalin's death was announced on March 6, 1953. In Moscow, however, surging crowds and tough security measures caused thousands of deaths.

Military officers were also weeping at the statue this morning, according to Pyongyang radio and television reports. That was yet a further sign that Kim Jong-il was consolidating his power base, since there had been rumors that the powerful military would not support Mr. Kim.

The television reports showed Kim Jong-il with an expression of grief on his face and occasionally he could be seen removing his eyeglasses to daub his eyes. In other scenes, thousands of North Koreans were shown descending upon a huge statue of Kim Il-sung in central Pyongyang, crying and throwing themselves on the ground.

In the footage broadcast in Seoul, South Korea, King Jong-il could be seen bowing solemnly to this father, whose body was surrounded by shoals of flowers.

Several top North Korean military figures, wearing black armbands, accompanied Kim Jong-il, another tacit signal that the military, North Korea's most powerful institution, was throwing its weight behind him.

The Communist Party daily newspaper, Rodong Sinmun, also declared Mr. Kim as the new leader.

The four diplomats in Pyongyang, all of whom spoke on the condition that neither they nor their countries be identified, said they had heard nothing specific about who would be the nation's new leader. But they all said it was obvious from newspaper and television reports there that Kim Jong-il was in control.

SUMMIT TALKS POSTPONED

Still, much about the future path of the secretive nation remains unknown. This morning, in a terse one-sentence announcement, North Korea notified South Korea that it was postponing indefinitely the first-ever summit meeting between the two nations, which was supposed to have taken place in Pyongyang from July 25 to July 27.

Talks with the United States on North Korea's nuclear program have also been suspended for now, although American officials have expressed optimism that the talks can be resumed some time after the funeral of Kim Il-sung, which was scheduled for Sunday.

Little is known about Kim Jong-il, the eldest son of Kim Il-sung. There have been reports that he is a playboy and an erratic manager, without the charisma of his father. He has studiously avoided meeting with foreign visitors, including former President Jimmy Carter, who was in North Korea recently. Even diplomats in Pyongyang have rarely if ever seen him. And since his father's death, Kim Jong-il has not appeared live on television in Pyongyang, according to diplomats there.

Hence his appearance tonight was a bit of a surprise. According to the Eastern European diplomat, the heads of mission of the roughly 25 embassies in Pyongyang were called to the presidential palace tonight, along with about 200 Korean officials.

After having to wait about two and a half hours, they were allowed into a room where the body of Kim Il-sung lies in state. The visitors stopped in front of the coffin, bowed their heads for a minute, and then went to offer condolences to other members of the family and other dignitaries.

Kim Jong-il, dressed in a dark Chinese-style suit, was at the head of the line. The visitors did not speak to him much, only offering their condolences quickly and receiving a thank you. "He was a normal man with a sad face," said the Eastern European diplomat.

The diplomat said that also in the receiving line were Mr. Kim's sister, his half brother, Kim Pyong Il, and O Jin U, the defense minister. The latter two have been considered possible rivals to Kim Jong-il.

North Korea has said that foreign leaders would not be invited to the funeral on Sunday. But the diplomats reached in Pyongyang today all said they expected that ambassadors stationed in North Korea would be able to attend the funeral, although they have not yet received invitations.

Blurred Images of North Korea's 'Junior'

BY ELAINE SCIOLINO | JULY 17, 1994

DEPENDING ON WHO is doing the talking, Kim Jong-il is a depraved movie fan who abuses women and alcohol; a terrorist who masterminded the 1983 bombing of the South Korean Cabinet and the 1987 midair bombing of a South Korean airliner; an awkward, misunderstood technocrat who longs to be a statesman, or all, some or none of the above.

The sharply divergent views underscore the scarcity of reliable information about the portly 52-year-old who has begun to emerge as North Korea's new leader, a man American intelligence officials still refer to as "junior" or "the kid."

President Clinton sounded as baffled as everyone else when he was asked about Mr. Kim last Monday, three days after the death of his father, Kim Il-sung, the world's longest-ruling dictator. "I don't know the younger Kim," Mr. Clinton said. "And I think you have to be careful in judging people by what others say about them one way or the other."

Kim-watchers spun themselves into an analytical frenzy overnight when the funeral of the father, set for Sunday, was suddenly postponed. But by this morning, officials in Seoul suggested that the succession was on track.

Mr. Kim's prospects, character and personal habits would hardly matter if the stakes were not so high for both Asia and the world. For he appears to be taking over what the Clinton Administration says is a rogue regime that may already have one or two nuclear bombs.

Few outsiders have ever met him, and he has rarely traveled outside the country. Much of what is said to be known about him is suspect because it comes from defectors whose views have been filtered through South Korean intelligence. When foreign visitors ask to meet him, as former President Jimmy Carter did during his recent trip, they are told he is out among the people in the countryside.

Both American and South Korean intelligence officials are so in the dark about Mr. Kim that they are reduced to analyzing frames from North Korean television of such seemingly minor details as changes in his weight, his elevator shoes, his pompadour hairdo and a sometimes drooping lower lip.

The information void has sparked a ferocious debate within the Administration — both between the State Department and the Central Intelligence Agency and within the C.I.A. itself — over who he is, what his intentions are and whether he will be able to fill the vast political vacuum left by his father's death.

The more benign view, shared by the State Department and some analysts in the C.I.A., is that while Mr. Kim may be eccentric, he has run the day-to-day operations of the country for some time, is now clearly in charge and may emerge eventually as a responsible leader.

The other view, shared by much of the C.I.A. and the Pentagon establishment, is that Mr. Kim is a Stalinist killer like his father. But because, unlike his father, he is not a national hero and does not have the respect of officials of the older generation or much of the military, he will be unable to make concessions on his country's nuclear program and lacks the charisma and standing to survive politically.

The backbiting has become so intense that different bureaus and agencies have inundated policymakers with hundreds of pages of often-contradictory analyses. "The situation we've gotten ourselves into can only be described as nutty," a longtime Korea watcher said.

A GRACIOUS HOST OPEN TO THE U.S.

A few close-up, if isolated, snapshots of Mr. Kim exist.

An Italian businessman, Carlo Baeli, describes Mr. Kim as a gentle soul, solicitous of his guests, curious about business and politics, and eager to have good relations with the United States.

"The thing that struck me most about him was his simplicity," Mr. Baeli said of a five-hour encounter on the Korean's yacht in September 1992. "He was very simple in how he met me, simple through the meal we had, simple when he said goodbye. He's very versatile and has a good sense of humor. Once the world meets the man, they'll realize that he's not the man described up to now."

Mr. Baeli, 61, the president of a Rome-based exporting company, Compagnia Internationale Scambi con l'Estero, has a $120 million contract to sell finishing machinery for marble and gold to North Korea. He may not be the most objective witness, but he is one of the only ones.

Dining on fish antipasto and grilled shrimp, drinking Hennessy brandy and French wine aboard the yacht, the two men toasted their friendship and mused about the world as military and political aides stood by, Mr. Baeli said.

"He asked first about the Italian economy, how things were going in Italy," Mr. Baeli said this week in a telephone interview from Rome. "Since we also have a Moscow office, he asked of my impressions of Russia. His sentiments toward the United States seemed to be very good. He wanted to have direct ties to the United States and not ties through other countries.

"He said they, the North Koreans, were ready and open to collaborate with the United States, and that they were already collaborating on research into Americans who died during the Korean War. He said: 'We are men and sooner or later we should come to an understanding. There is no reason for us to be enemies of the United States.' "

At one point, Mr. Kim was concerned that his guest might be tired, so he asked an aide to bring them fishing rods and they fished off the side of the yacht. As the afternoon wore on, Mr. Baeli said, "We spoke of work, politics, music, theater.

"We spoke mainly of the shows put on in North Korea where up to 5,000 characters are on stage. Apparently Kim is the inspiration of these shows."

SELF-CONSCIOUSNESS AND BOYISH BRAVADO

Choe Eun Hee, a well-known South Korean actress, and her husband, Shin Sang Ok, a filmmaker, have a different view. The two, who say

But the formal rise to power of Kim Jong-il suggests that the mourning period for the father has now ended, and the younger Mr. Kim has dropped some tantalizing hints that changes may now be in order.

The South Korean Government issued a statement that seemed to express a cautious welcome to Mr. Kim, voicing hope that his election would increase stability in North Korea and lead to improvements in relations between the two countries.

"We've always been aware that North Korea was under the control of Mr. Kim Jong-il before this official announcement," a senior South Korean Government official said today. "But now that he will have the actual post of head of the party, the North Korean Government may be more stable, more responsible and more predictable."

The position of President has also been vacant since the death of Kim Il-sung, and it is unclear whether Kim Jong-il will later assume that post as well.

North Korea is in many ways less a Communist state than a reincarnation of an ancient Korean kingdom, in which the ruler's mandate is based not on political mechanisms but on birthright and Confucian loyalties. Thus while it might have seemed odd elsewhere in the Communist world for a son to inherit power from his father or for the nation's top leadership posts to be left empty for three years after the death of a ruler, both patterns are borrowed directly from Korean history.

Similarly, the Korean press has lately described phenomena like trees blossoming out of season, which to Westerners may seem an odd thing to make a fuss over but is understandable to Korean traditionalists as a sign that the Mandate of Heaven is passing.

"On the morning of Sept. 22, fishermen of the fishery station in Rajin-Sonbong City caught a 10-centimeter long white sea cucumber while fishing on the waters off Chongjin," the official New Korea News Agency reported. "They said the rare white sea cucumber has come to hail the auspicious event of electing comrade Kim Jong-il as party general secretary."

"Seeing the mysterious natural phenomena," the agency continued, "Koreans say comrade Kim Jong-il is indeed the greatest of great men produced by Heaven and that flowers come into bloom to mark the great event."

Mr. Kim has often been portrayed, particularly by South Koreans, as little more than a playboy terrorist with a passion for films. But some scholars say that Kim Jong-il has a more serious side, and in the last few years he has presided over a modest economic liberalization, with invitations for foreign investment and a growing number of private markets emerging in the countryside for food and clothing.

In a remarkable series of tape recordings smuggled out of North Korea, Mr. Kim can be heard admitting that centrally planned economies do not work as well as the market. Moreover, in a major essay published in August — largely ignored because it was long, dreary and full of slogans — Mr. Kim gave the clearest indication that he might pursue more flexible policies.

"Improving the relations between the North and the South is an urgent requirement," Mr. Kim wrote. He called for putting into effect long-frozen accords between the two Koreas and expressed willingness to negotiate with South Korea and also improve relations with Japan and the United States.

North Koreans Officially Inherit Another 'Great Leader'

BY NICHOLAS D. KRISTOF | SEPT. 6, 1998

NORTH KOREA today became the first Communist country to transfer government power within a family dynasty, as it formally anointed Marshal Kim Jong-il as its "Great Leader" and chairman of an expanded National Defense Commission.

In effect, Mr. Kim, the eldest son of former "Great Leader" Kim Il-sung, who died four years ago, will govern in much the style of an ancient Korean king, ruling absolutely and inheriting legitimacy not from institutions but from the bloodline of the previous ruler.

Tonight's announcement said Kim Jong-il's position as Defense Commission chairman was "the highest post of the state," but did not specify what would happen to the presidency. There have been reports that it will be abolished and the honor held forever by Mr. Kim's late father.

The consolidation of power by Kim Jong-il ends the four-year interregnum left by the death of Kim Il-sung. The younger Mr. Kim had already assumed the top positions in the ruling Communist Party and the army, and now he in effect adds a job as head of the state.

Most analysts expect few immediate changes because Mr. Kim has already been running North Korea since his father's death. But some say the coronation of a new king permits the country to experiment carefully with new policies.

"He's less ideological than his father, and he represents a different generation," said Han S. Park, a political scientist at the University of Georgia who regularly visits North Korea.

North Korea now refers to Mr. Kim as "Great Leader" in its English-language documents instead of the "Dear Leader" title he carried while his father was alive. But the Korean expressions used are still different from the one that was reserved for his father, although the younger Mr. Kim is hailed in terms that could scarcely be grander.

"He is an outstanding thinker and theoretician, a distinguished statesman and a peerlessly brilliant commander who has ushered in a heyday of the era of the Workers Party, an era of great prosperity of socialist Korea," the official Korean Central News Agency declared tonight.

If North Korea is one of the most perplexing of nations, Kim Jong-il is among the most mysterious of leaders. Intelligence experts believe that he may have several nuclear weapons, making him the least understood of any leader with a finger on a nuclear trigger.

Mr. Kim, 56, has traveled outside his country only once, to China in 1983, and has never met a non-Communist. Although he is hailed in North Korea as a virtual deity, his voice has been broadcast only once, when a television clip showed him addressing a military parade with a brief slogan: "Glory be to the heroic officers and men of the Korean People's Army!"

Some analysts see him as a maniac, noting that he has been accused of kidnapping a South Korean actor-and-actress couple whose work he admired, of planning the bombing of the South Korean Cabinet in 1983, and of plotting the bombing of a civilian South Korean airliner in 1987. A woman who planted the bomb, Kim Ilyon Hee, said Kim Jong-il had ordered the bombing.

Others say that he lacks his father's charisma but appears to be intelligent and relatively open-minded. Tape-recordings of private conversations in which he frankly acknowledges the economic inefficiency of socialism were smuggled out of North Korea several years ago, and a defector who claims to have lived in his house says Mr. Kim worked hard, had a computer on his desk and watched CNN and other foreign television networks.

That defector, Lee Nam Ok, who is now living in hiding in Europe, told a Japanese magazine that she never saw any sign that Mr. Kim was a temperamental playboy, as he is sometimes described. She recounted Mr. Kim's life in his compound as luxurious, with air conditioning and a huge playroom full of slot machines and other toys for his son to play with, and she said he had sent his son to a boarding school in Switzerland to gain exposure to the outside world.

In a remarkably moderate essay last year, Mr. Kim called for improved relations with South Korea and the United States. But then, he presumably was also behind a series of commando missions in which submarines dropped off troops on the South's shores, and he has resisted calls for a summit meeting by the South's President, Kim Dae Jung.

North Korea remains the most mobilized and rigidly controlled society in the world. But in recent years, there have been signs of change in North Korea, including the emergence of small-scale free markets in some towns, and the country has also sought foreign investment.

In some ways, the effective abolition of the presidency complicates an already muddy picture at what seems to be a crucial time in North Korean history. Millions of North Koreans are widely believed to be on the edge of starvation, and the economy has largely collapsed because of energy shortages, mismanagement and natural disasters.

There are widely diverging estimates of the seriousness of the food shortages. By all accounts, hunger is widespread and is causing some deaths, but some estimates are that the death toll is modest while others range up to the millions.

North Korea refuses visits by most foreigners, so it is difficult to gauge the true level of suffering.

A landmark agreement reached in 1994, under which North Korea agreed to give up its nuclear program in exchange for energy from the West, now appears to be in jeopardy because of recriminations and ill feeling on both sides. If that agreement is completely breached, North Korea may revive its nuclear program, leading to a renewed confrontation between North Korea and Western powers.

Western scholars say Mr. Kim was born in a camp in the Soviet Union, where his father was based as a guerrilla fighting the Japanese

NOBORU HASHIMOTO/SYGMA/GETTY IMAGES

Kim Jong-il celebrates the 50th Anniversary of the Workers' Party of Korea (WPK).

forces then occupying Korea. But North Korea says Mr. Kim was born on Mount Paektu, a sacred mountain in Korean history.

North Korea has often claimed magical associations with Mr. Kim. Last fall, when he was appointed leader of the ruling Workers Party, the official news media announced that flowers suddenly bloomed and that a magical white sea cucumber entered a fisherman's net "to hail the auspicious event" of Mr. Kim's rise.

"Seeing the mysterious natural phenomena, Koreans say Comrade Kim Jong-il is indeed the greatest of great men produced by heaven and that flowers come into bloom to mark the great event," the official news agency declared at the time.

Inside the Mind of North Korea's 'Dear Leader': First, Pay Attention. And Then Pay Up.

BY NICHOLAS D. KRISTOF | SEPT. 6, 1998

SO I FINALLY GOT the world's attention! The United States and Japan thought they could ignore me and — kersplash — I send one missile shooting over Japan, and finally they look in my direction. Ha! Maybe I should do this more often!

And then they call me irrational. Can't they see that this was the only rational thing to do? If I didn't scare them every now and then, they would ignore me totally and I'd be like Fidel Castro, a nothing.

Look at me! The imperialists tried to bully me back in 1994, telling me I had to stop my nuclear program. But I was ready to go to war with them, and so they decided to save lives and chicken out. We reached a big agreement: I would freeze my program and the Americans and the other countries would give me free heating oil and build me a $4 billion light-water nuclear reactor. You've got to be pushy.

YANKEE DOUBLE-CROSS

Of course, the Americans tried to double-cross me. Despite their agreement, they wouldn't lift most of their sanctions, they lagged in building the new reactor, they delayed shipping me oil and they didn't even think about normalizing relations.

I was ready to get rid of my whole missile program in exchange for the right payoff, but they wouldn't cough up the kind of dough I was talking about. They wouldn't pay me money and they wouldn't pay attention.

Well, now maybe they'll pay something! If my nuclear program got them to give me a $4 billion reactor and free oil, think what my missile program should be worth — especially since the Central Intelligence

Agency thinks I still have a few nukes that I just might figure out how to attach to a missile. The imperialists were worried about my old Nodong missiles, which couldn't even reach Tokyo. Well, they missed a bargain. Now they'll have to pay billions for my program, because I can take out anything in Japan. And if my engineers can improve the booster rocket, I'll be able to reach Alaska and Hawaii.

O.K., O.K., I know the missiles are hopelessly inaccurate. But so what if I aim for the Yankee base at Yokosuka and hit Tokyo instead? It just makes the Japanese more nervous than ever. And their fear is what gives me bargaining power.

GETTING PAID

Yeah, and think of all that free advertising I got. The Syrians and Iranians see Secretary of State yapping puppy Albright denounce my missiles, and they'll pay more than ever. I'll get paid off one way or another; by the Yankees for giving up my missile program or by the Syrians and Iranians for continuing it. These two-stage rockets can deliver a one-ton payload more than 1,000 miles, and Israel will be in the bombsights.

Of course, my Foreign Ministry is whining these days. The diplomats say we may have overplayed our hand, and they're worried now that Japan has cut off aid and flights to our country, now that the Yankee Congress is sniveling about whether to back away from the 1994 nuclear agreement. Huh! Wimps!

Washington will come through because it knows that it would be risking war if it didn't. Sure, I would lose. But I've got one thing in my favor: 10 million people within artillery range. Seoul will be a sea of flames. I have the guts to fight to lose, but the Yankees don't have the stomach to fight to win.

The imperialists don't really think I'd level Seoul, but they can't be sure. Sometimes it pays to be perceived as irrational, and sending a missile racing over Japan just adds to my credibility as a maniac. (And wasn't it a nice touch when we said later that the missile launched a scientific satellite transmitting immortal revolutionary hymns?)

Oh, yeah, sure, if the Yankees do cut off aid, then that will make it tougher here. But when things get really desperate, people will come running with aid. If people go hungry here, then the pressure is on Washington and Tokyo, not me.

I love to read what these foreign analysts say. They think North Korea is falling apart. It's just like those foreigners who thought China was falling apart in the early 1950's. But hunger doesn't make people rebel; it just makes them die.

In China, 30 million people died in Mao Zedong's famine of the early 1960's; there wasn't a peep of protest. Then Deng Xiaoping gave the Chinese people pork and rice and they tried to stage a revolution against him at Tiananmen Square.

I'll never make that mistake. I know that contact with barbarians or, worse, bourgeois democracy, destabilizes a country. I'll never open up my country the way Deng did.

Those arrogant foreigners think they can make life hard on us and change us. This is Korea! We're not weaklings. If we were compromisers our nation would have been absorbed by China or Japan a thousand years ago.

TOUGH TO BE KING

Two hundred years ago, King Yongjo knew his son would be a terrible heir, so he locked the weeping young man in a box in the courtyard and left him to die. It took 13 days. That's the toughness that it takes to be a king of Korea, and I've got that toughness.

The South Korean puppets have lost their strength, and we in the North are the only real Koreans left. That's why we have restored a dynasty, just like the ancients. My father died four years ago, and the foreigners all puzzled about why I didn't fill the vacancy and whether that meant I was weak. Don't they know about filial piety? If they had read Korean history, they would have known that a good Korean prince waits several years before succeeding his father. I'm not a Communist. I'm a Confucian.

Now it is my turn to succeed my father as President and party leader. I'll reform the economy and try to rely more on the market mechanism, because that's the only thing that works. But I'll never open up this country. I'll never risk losing control.

I will stand up to the foreigners and my people will stand behind me, as long as they have the strength to stand. I need enemies more than I need friends.

Ah, yes, what a lovely missile that was. It made me a few more enemies. They can despise me, insult me. But they'll have to respect me.

Poor little Castro. I should sell him a missile or two to launch over Florida. Then he would get some respect as well, and maybe some American foreign aid.

Visit Revises Image of North Korean

BY JANE PERLEZ | OCT. 26, 2000

WHEN SECRETARY OF STATE Madeleine K. Albright landed in North Korea this week, the Clinton administration had closely watched what it viewed as the erratic and threatening behavior of the leader, Kim Jong-il, for more than six years.

A series of crises that concerned the North Korean nuclear program and its ability to build and launch long-range missiles had driven Washington to believe that the reclusive Mr. Kim was determined to destabilize the North Asian region and, possibly, attack the United States.

After negotiating with Mr. Kim over two days, Dr. Albright and her team of North Korea specialists who left the country this morning said they had come away with a different impression. They found, they said, a leader who could be reasoned with and keeps up on events through the Internet and CNN and who has traveled to China, India and Russia.

The assessment of Mr. Kim toward the end of this visit is vastly more positive than it was several months ago, when there was considerable disbelief in Washington, and even some quiet scoffing, at similar descriptions given by President Kim Dae Jung of South Korea after his visit to North Korea in June.

In one of the many conversations with the secretary that ranged over subjects like his annual viewing of the Oscars — presumably by videotape — Mr. Kim said he was examining alternatives to his Communist economy. Specifically, he said he liked the Swedish model.

As the Americans try to fathom what has prompted what is apparently Mr. Kim's new readiness to abandon his missile program on conditions that would be acceptable to the United States, the central theme of the talks here, they have come up with two basic reasons: the economic survival of a country that is teetering on the brink of collapse and the survival of his own dictatorship.

"I think he's beginning to think about how to sustain his economy over time," a senior administration official said. "He has some understanding that missile exports, although they obviously bring in hard currency, also produce problems for him."

Most significantly, the official added, Mr. Kim apparently understood that maintaining a hard-line posture on his missile program and exports prevented any possibility of a relationship with the United States.

The Americans said they believed that Mr. Kim, who inherited the leadership from his father, Kim Il-sung, who died six years ago, needs to shore up his vulnerabilities. He runs a country where the 1.1 million-member military wields a disproportionate degree of authority. But as the indulged child of a powerful man, he never worked his way up through the ranks.

Whether Mr. Kim, whom officials said they found smart but far from being a creative thinker, will actually put into effect any economic changes remains a question. Improving the economy would mean opening the country to foreign investors, much as China has done. But that is a move that could produce profound shocks in one of the most isolated countries in the world.

Asked whether Mr. Kim understood the implications of opening his society to the Internet and a global economy, the administration official replied, "I think that is, in part, why this will be a slow process."

In preparing for Dr. Albright's visit here, possibly the prelude to a trip by President Clinton before he leaves office, Washington has had to build on the little that it knows about Mr. Kim. At home, his life story is murky and subject to wild rumors.

Despite hagiography that insists that he was born in a log cabin on a legendary mountaintop, American officials said they believed that Mr. Kim was born in a military camp in the Far East of the Soviet Union in 1942, when his father was fighting Japanese troops. Mr. Kim's father moved back to Korea at the end of World War II, heading the Korean Communist Party in the Soviet-occupied North and becoming

CHAPTER 5

Leading the "Axis of Evil"

In 2002, U.S.-North Korea relations took a turn from rocky to hostile when U.S. President George W. Bush declared North Korea part of an "axis of evil" — nations sponsoring terrorism or engaged in the development of nuclear weapons. However, unlike in Iraq, to which Bush's "war on terror" brought U.S. troops, little progress was made in terms of détente by the time Kim Jong-il died in 2011. Meanwhile, Kim ensured his regime's continuity, grooming his son Kim Jong-un for the nation's top post.

Choosing The Right Enemies

OPINION | BY MICHAEL O'HANLON | FEB. 6, 2002

IN HIS STATE OF THE UNION ADDRESS, President Bush took aim at what he called an "axis of evil" — countries like Iraq, Iran and North Korea together with their terrorist associates. He implied that the United States might take strong action against all parts of this global collection of unpalatable actors.

However, Mr. Bush is wrong to lump these countries and terrorist groups together. We will harm our security if we fail to appreciate the great differences among them.

This is particularly true of North Korea and its tyrannical ruler, Kim Jong-il. North Korea remains heavily armed and threatening, and largely as a result of its excessive military spending, its citizens are extremely poor. But for all its flaws, the North Korean regime is not like Saddam Hussein's Iraq. We can work with Kim Jong-il — provided that we are smart about how we do it.

Consider how much things improved in the years before Mr. Bush took office. Until 1994, North Korea appeared on its way to developing a sizable nuclear arsenal. In 1998, it fired a three-stage rocket over Japan, suggesting it might soon develop an intercontinental missile capable of delivering weapons of mass destruction against the United States. Not long ago, American intelligence officers considered Korea the world's most dangerous flash point, with the likelihood that any outbreak of war would lead to thousands of American deaths and hundreds of thousands of Korean casualties.

By the end of 2000, the situation had improved on almost all fronts. In 1994, the Clinton administration worked out a deal for shutting down and monitoring North Korea's major nuclear facilities. That "agreed framework," which has held to this day, called for South Korea, Japan and the United States to provide North Korea with fuel oil to replace the energy that the nuclear reactors would have produced — and, eventually, to build North Korea new nuclear reactors with less capability for contributing to a nuclear weapons program.

More recently, the United States convinced North Korea to impose a moratorium on long-range missile testing in exchange for a lifting of most trade sanctions and an improvement in diplomatic contacts. That moratorium also continues to hold. And a process of détente began as well, including a meeting in 2000 between the leaders of the two Koreas.

North Korea's support for terrorism has declined drastically in recent years; there is no evidence the regime actively supports major terrorist organizations. Even so, all is not well on the Korean peninsula. North Korea remains hypermilitarized; it still exports missiles and other arms, though in far smaller quantities than a decade ago; it may still be quietly working on its long-range missile program; it might even have a "basement bomb" project to develop nuclear arms. Its economy remains a shambles. And, since Mr. Bush took office and showed little support for the "sunshine policy" of South Korea's president, Kim Dae Jung, toward the North, the process of détente has essentially been frozen.

What to do? The Bush administration resists the idea, preferred by some in the Clinton administration, of simply buying out North Korea's missile programs. For this administration, that smacks of blackmail and could encourage extortionate behavior from Pyongyang. But the Bush administration has failed to offer a serious alternative to Mr. Clinton's policy. Threatening rhetoric does not amount to a policy and may actually increase the chances of war on the peninsula.

Rather than merely buying out North Korea's missile program, the United States and its allies should insist that North Korea accept an arms control regime that would scale back conventional weaponry on the peninsula. If North Korea were willing to begin economic reform, perhaps along a Chinese model, the United States, Japan and South Korea should commit to providing substantial economic assistance — not as bribery, but as genuine aid to help convert the North Korean economy.

What will not work is treating Kim Jong-il like Saddam Hussein or Mullah Omar. As bad as Mr. Kim may be, he has displayed some recognition that he needs to improve relations with the outside world. He can possibly be coaxed, but probably not bludgeoned. As he prepares for a trip to South Korea in less than two weeks, Mr. Bush needs to make sure that he wields both a carrot and a stick in his dealings with Pyongyang — a combination that has worked well in recent years.

MICHAEL O'HANLON is a senior fellow at the Brookings Institution.

The Obsessions of Kim Jong-il

OPINION | BY B. R. MYERS | MAY 19, 2003

THERE WAS A TIME when the specter of communism frightened Americans into digging bomb shelters in their backyards. Today, improbably enough, the frequent characterization of North Korea as a Stalinist or hard-line Communist nation appears to be having a calming effect, perhaps because it evokes a happy time when all America's enemies were cold-hearted materialists who could therefore be reasoned with.

If it takes misperceptions to get everyone talking, then maybe they're not such a bad thing. But it would be dangerous for America to believe that it has negotiated successfully with Kim Jong-il's kind before. Mr. Kim is not a Stalinist in any relevant sense, and his party's "juche" ideology has nothing in common with the Soviet-style communism his father espoused during the Korean War.

Granted, the red-themed birthday parades may look familiar, but the cult of the two Kims is no socialist personality cult. Stalin and Mao were revered for their perfect grasp of dialectical materialism, an omnipotent science that made them omnipotent too. Kim Jong-il and his late father, Kim Il-sung, are revered, like the monarchs they more closely resemble, for their perfect embodiment of national virtues.

Chief among these virtues is "sobak ham," a hard-to-translate Korean term that corresponds closely to the word spontaneity in its Marxist-Leninist sense. The Soviets considered the spontaneity of the common people, especially their tendency to violence, to be a dangerous force unless tempered with political consciousness. In North Korea, the people's spontaneity is seen as one of the country's greatest strengths.

North Korean novels and movies often show the hero casting off the restraints of his book learning in a fit of wild, sometimes suicidal rage against the Japanese or American enemy. This political culture induces officials to tolerate a high level of violence in daily life; North

Korean refugees attest that fistfights are the accepted way for men and women to settle even minor differences.

While communism was always an internationalist movement, juche (literally, self-reliance) sees the world in ethnic terms. North Korean propaganda makes no distinction between American capitalists and American workers; the entire "Yankee" race is presented as inherently evil, degenerate and ugly. Dictionaries and textbooks suggest that Americans be described with bestial attributes ("snout" for nose, for example).

The central villain of Han Sorya's novella "Jackals" (1951), the country's most enduring work of fiction, tells of an American child who beats a Korean boy so brutally that he ends up in a hospital — where he is murdered by the American's missionary parents. Since the South Korean government began pursuing its policy of rapprochement, the North's ethnocentric world view has become even more stark; the United States is now presented as being exclusively responsible for all tensions on the peninsula.

This propaganda appears to be effective even among North Koreans opposed to the rule of Kim Jong-il. When I visited a resettlement center for refugees near Seoul last year, many of those to whom I was introduced as an American recoiled in terror or glared at me in hatred.

The glorification of spontaneous violence, sweeping hatred of the American people, and a budding nuclear capacity: The combination is liable, as P. G. Wodehouse would say, to start a train of thought. Perhaps some in Washington can sleep better by believing that Kim Jong-il has an urbane and sensible take on the political culture he inherited from his father in 1994. But none other than Mr. Kim was at the head of the party's propaganda apparatus when it went into overdrive in the mid- to late 1960's. Too much is made of his much-publicized love of pizza and Hollywood videos; while his hedonism may make him a hypocrite, it's highly unlikely that it signifies any real affection for the West.

In short, Mr. Kim stands for more than just a desire to stay in power. America should focus less on his eccentricities and more on his ideology, especially since the anti-Americanism at its core is as heartfelt and popular as the anti-Americanism that led to 9/11 and other terrorist attacks. Diplomacy cannot succeed until the Bush administration begins addressing the historical basis for this hatred.

A good start would be a public apology for the excesses of the American air campaign in the Korean War: the saturation bombing of North Korean cities, the use of napalm, the attacks on irrigation dams in order to cause flooding. At the same time, President Bush should call on Mr. Kim to stop posturing about the "axis of evil" remark, which was tame compared with what North Korea's official press has been saying for the past few years about the United States, Pyongyang's main aid donor.

It is time for the president to demand that North Korea's official news media accord the same basic civility to Washington as to Seoul. In an isolated nation dominated by propaganda, this would be a significant sign that Mr. Kim is serious about wanting to improve relations.

The Last Emperor

BY PETER MAASS | OCT. 19, 2003

THE DEAR LEADER is a workaholic. Kim Jong-il sleeps four hours a night, or if he works through the night, as he sometimes does, he sleeps four hours a day. His office is a hive of activity; reports cross his desk at all hours. Dressed as always in his signature khaki jumpsuit, he reads them all, issuing instructions to aides, dashing off handwritten notes or picking up the phone at 3 a.m. and telling subordinates what should lead the news broadcasts or whom to dispatch to a prison camp. His micromanaging style is less Caligula, with whom he has often been compared, and more Jimmy Carter on an authoritarian tear.

The Dear Leader, as the North Korean media refer to him, wishes to be viewed as a modern leader. He has boasted to visitors that he has three computers in his office, though it's not known if he operates them himself or has aides who do so. His eldest son is reputed to be a computer whiz and, like sons the world over, is credited with bringing his father into the digital age. When Madeleine K. Albright, then the secretary of state, visited North Korea in 2000, Kim asked her, as he said farewell, to give him the State Department's e-mail address.

Because of weakening eyesight, the Dear Leader rarely reads newspapers; for keeping abreast of world affairs, he relies on television. It is a safe bet that he is well aware of the uproar caused by his government's confirmation, earlier this month, that it has begun making nuclear bombs from reprocessed plutonium. In a meeting a few years ago with a group of South Korean media executives, Kim explained that he began watching South Korean television in 1979. A media junkie, he also watches NHK from Japan, as well as CCTV from China and CNN. Having led his nation into chronic poverty and famine, what does he make of the enormous wealth he sees in the broadcasts and commercials?

Ordinary North Koreans would be sent to the gulag for watching Western TV, but the Dear Leader may do as he pleases, as all dictators may do as they please, and it pleases him to watch television. He especially enjoys watching tapes of the latest movies from Hollywood, some of which are believed to be sent to Pyongyang in diplomatic pouches from North Korean missions in New York and Beijing.

Kim is not known to speak Japanese or Chinese, so interpreters presumably assist him with foreign-language broadcasts; on any given evening, his interpreter might be his favorite mistress, Ko Young Hee, who was born in Japan and is assumed to speak Japanese. When Kim watches Russian television, as he says he does, he may not need an interpreter, because he spent his early years in the Soviet Union; when Russians visit, he sings them Soviet military songs. As for English, he knows at least a few words. A Japanese man who worked as Kim's personal chef wrote in a recent memoir that the Dear Leader always asked for extra helpings of toro, his favorite cut of sushi, by saying "one more" in English.

The Dear Leader has always been a master of details. Although it was not until 1994, upon the death of his father, Kim Il-sung, that Kim Jong-il became the official ruler of North Korea, he was all but running the country for years before that. Appointments to any senior post were made by him, whether in the Korean Workers Party (which controls all government institutions) or the Korean People's Army. Decisions on all manner of issues — from the gifts of food and electronic goods that party officials and commoners received on national holidays to the direction and scope of the country's clandestine nuclear-weapons programs — were made by "the party center," as Kim was called, in whispers, in the years before his father's death. The choicest reward that he doled out was a Mercedes-Benz with a license plate that begins "2-16," in reference to his birthday, Feb. 16.

The Dear Leader's political skills, underestimated by foreign observers until recently, are beginning to register now that he has begun meeting foreigners on a regular basis and now that his regime, along with Iran, is one of two surviving members of the "axis of evil" proclaimed by President Bush. Albright's delegation spent more than 12 hours with Kim over two days in October 2000, half of that time in negotiations and the other half at dinners and ceremonial functions. During one negotiating session, Kim was presented with a list of 14 technical questions related to his missile program; the Americans expected him to pass the list to advisers who would respond later. Instead, Kim went down the list, one question after another, and answered most of them himself.

Indeed, the Dear Leader, who turned 62 this year, knows quite a bit about the world around him. And after decades of being nearly clueless, the world around him is gradually getting to know the Dear Leader, too.

The Bush administration is trying to figure out how to end Kim's regime, or at least to neutralize it. This is proving to be an extraordinarily difficult task, since the regime is far more resilient than anyone expected and far more dangerous.

North Korea has possessed short-range missiles for years, but was never known to have long-range missile capability. Then in 1998 North Korea stunned the intelligence community by launching a three-stage rocket bearing a satellite. The C.I.A. says that it believes these Taepodong-1 rockets could be used as missiles to reach the United States. The rocket veered off course after launch, so the North Koreans obviously have some kinks to work out. Even so, Washington is worried, not only about North Korea being able to launch an intercontinental attack but also about the North Koreans selling their missile technology to other regimes. North Korea is believed to have provided missiles to Pakistan in exchange for nuclear technology. And according to a recently released report by David Kay, the C.I.A. adviser on weapons of mass destruction in Iraq, North Korea agreed in 1999 to a missile deal with Baghdad that was aborted late last year.

No one is sure of North Korea's own nuclear intentions. In 1994, facing the threat of a pre-emptive attack by the United States, North

Korea agreed to freeze its nuclear program in exchange for a package of foreign aid and energy supplies. At the time, the C.I.A. publicly estimated that North Korea might already possess an atom bomb. The 1994 agreement fell apart in 2002 after North Korea kicked out U.N. nuclear inspectors who were keeping watch over 8,000 plutonium rods that could be reprocessed into weapons-grade material.

During the past year, North Korea strongly hinted that the rods were being reprocessed, and on Oct. 2 the regime announced, more directly than before, that the reprocessing was under way and that its "nuclear deterrent force" was being expanded. Experts say that if all 8,000 rods are reprocessed, North Korea could make perhaps 20 nuclear bombs, but it's not certain whether bombs have yet been made; bluffing is an integral element of Kim's nuclear poker game.

Along with South Korea, Japan, China and Russia, the United States began the first round of so-called six-party talks in Beijing with North Korea in late August, and a second round may be held in November. Whether those talks take place, and what happens if they do, depends greatly on whether the Bush administration decides to offer incentives for Kim to disarm or whether it decides to isolate him further. The underlying issues are quite stark: Can Kim be reformed? Can he be deposed? At the heart of the matter is this: Who is Kim Jong-il?

Dictators come in different strains, like poisons. Some are catastrophically toxic; others, less so. Quite often, the harm a dictator will cause is associated with an internal drive to violence or a paranoia that begets violence or a mixture of both. Saddam Hussein is a case in point; his personal viciousness is legendary. Dictators of this sort are easy to read and easy to despise because they are obvious killers.

But what is to be made of a dictator who is charming, as Kim can be, and has never been known personally to raise a weapon or even a hand against anyone? This can be a no-less-dangerous strain of dictator, and in the world today, Kim Jong-il is its most striking example. Though friendly with important visitors, Kim is vicious to his own people. An estimated two million of them died during a preventable famine in the 1990's, and several hundred thousand are in prison and labor camps; many have been executed.

While I was a reporter in South Korea, from 1987 to 1990, it was common to view Kim as an erratic playboy; tales of his reclusiveness and tastes for women and wine were abundant. He was, it seemed, a nut job, incapable of holding North Korea together once his father died. While Kim Il-sung was alive, Kim Jong-il avoided the spotlight. North Koreans did not even hear his voice until a broadcast in 1992, when at a ceremony for the army's 60th anniversary, he said, "Glory to the people's heroic military!" Six words. It would be many years before he was heard from again.

Kim Jong-il has never granted an interview to a Western reporter, and visits to North Korea by Western journalists are exceedingly rare. (I visited Pyongyang in 1989 but was refused a visa this time around.) However, since 2000 a flood of information has emerged from South Koreans, Russians and Americans who have met the Dear Leader and from high-level defectors who have escaped his orbit. What emerges from these sources is a picture of a dictator who is not crazy like Idi Amin or bloodthirsty like Saddam Hussein. Kim can be courteous, he is very intelligent and he doesn't drink nearly as much as he is rumored to. Nor is he the playboy that the popular myth makes him out to be. Instead, his dictatorship mixes high technology with Confucian traditions: a kind of cyberfeudalism. It is an ideology that has been catastrophic for the people of North Korea.

It was the summer of 2000, and Kim Jong-il was in a sunny mood. He had just held a summit meeting in Pyongyang with Kim Dae Jung, South Korea's president at the time. The South Koreans, in order to make the meeting happen, had provided $100 million in under-the-table payments, which meant North Korea's usually bare treasury was temporarily not so bare. The cash had created a brief thaw in relations, and on Aug. 5 a delegation of South Korean media executives, including the heads of its television networks and newspapers, arrived at Pyongyang airport.

On their first night in North Korea's capital, the visitors from Seoul were treated to a feast at a banquet hall. Wine from Bordeaux was served, along with multiple courses of Korean food, including kalbi-kuk, a meat stew. The guests ate with copper chopsticks, and their dinner lasted for four hours, presided over at the head table by the Dear Leader. Seated to his right was Choe Hak Rae, then publisher of Hankyoreh Shinmun, a newspaper known for its friendly coverage of North Korea.

As Choe recalls, Kim was ebullient, acting more like a Broadway producer with a smash hit on his hands than a dictator running a repressive and impoverished regime. Kim told jokes and casually conversed about everything from horses to missiles. When a fawning aide stopped by the head table and began praising his boss, Kim told him to skip the formalities — his precise words, in Korean, were "Cut it out" — and pour wine for their brothers from South Korea. He cried out "Straight!" when it came time for a toast, meaning that they should drain their glasses, but he only sipped his own wine. Kim told his guests that his doctors had suggested he cut down on liquor. Dictators can do many things, but they cannot keep their livers young forever.

The conversation turned to hobbies. Kim is an avid equestrian and told Choe that his best thoughts occur on horseback. He prefers Orlovs, a Russian breed, and likes to ride them as fast and as far as they can go.

The subject of war was raised, delicately. Why, Choe inquired, was North Korea's government spending its scarce resources on ballistic missiles instead of education or other social programs that would directly benefit its starving citizens? The Dear Leader did not hesitate to reply. "The missiles cannot reach the United States," he said, "and if I launch them, the U.S. would fire back thousands of missiles and we would not survive. I know that very well. But I have to let them know I have missiles. I am making them because only then will the United States talk to me."

The North Korean leader took a liking to Choe and invited him to return with his family, offering to show them around and ride horses with them. When Choe left Pyongyang a few days later, Kim shook his hand at a farewell luncheon and said, with great emotion: "Keep your promise. Come next spring with your family."

Choe has not returned — the North-South thaw has chilled a bit — but North Korean officials have passed on to him a stream of entreaties from the Dear Leader. The gist of the messages, according to Choe, whom I met in Seoul in August, is quite simple: "Why haven't you come?"

According to the official version of his life story, Kim was born on Feb. 16, 1942, in a log cabin on Mount Paektu, the highest mountain on the Korean Peninsula. When he was born, the official version goes, the sky was brightened by a star and a double rainbow.

The truth is that Kim was born a year earlier in the Soviet Union, at an army base near Khabarovsk, in the Soviet far east, not far from the short border shared by the two countries. His father was stationed there as the commander of a Korean battalion in the Soviet Army 88th Brigade, which engaged in reconnaissance missions against Japanese troops. Because it would be inconvenient, for reasons of Korean nationalism, to have Kim born on foreign soil, his place and date of birth have been fabricated in official biographies.

The biographers also make no mention of Kim's childhood name — Yura, which is Russian and was used through his high-school years. Kim had a younger brother who also had a Russian nickname, Shura. In 1945, after Japan was defeated and the northern half of Korea occupied by Soviet troops, Kim Il-sung was taken to Pyongyang by his Soviet benefactors and installed as the leader of North Korea. (The official version has Kim Il-sung heroically leading Korean guerrillas in a rout of the Japanese.) A few months later, the boys moved to Pyongyang, where their younger sister, Kim Kyung Hee, was born.

Shura died in 1948 in a drowning accident while swimming in a pond with Kim Jong-il. In 1949, Kim's mother, Kim Jong Sook, died while giving birth to a stillborn child. Though well cared for — their father, after all, was North Korea's leader — Kim Jong-il and his little sister became de facto orphans: their mother dead, their father busy laying the groundwork for his socialist paradise. In 1950, the Korean War broke out, and the children were sent to the safety of Manchuria, where they stayed until the war ended in 1953. Kim was learning to survive on his own, which meant using his wits.

Back in Pyongyang, he attended Namsan Senior High School, where the ruling elite's children were educated; he often rode a motorcycle to class. Even then, he was a student of power. According to Hwang Jang Yop, who was a top aide to Kim Il-sung, the younger Kim showed an early interest in politics. (Hwang defected from North Korea in 1997, so his memoir, published in South Korea, is hardly an official hagiography.) In 1959 Hwang accompanied Kim Il-sung to Moscow, and although Kim Jong-il was only a senior in high school, he went along, too.

"Kim Jong-il was intelligent and full of curiosity, asking me many questions," Hwang wrote. "Despite his young age, he already harbored political ambitions. He paid special attention to his father. … Every morning he would help his father to get up and put on his shoes." In the evening, Hwang wrote, when Kim Il-sung returned from a day of official meetings, Kim Jong-il assembled his father's staff "and had them report to him about the things that happened during the day. He then proceeded to give orders."

In 1964, Kim graduated with a degree in political economy from Kim Il-sung University, an elite institution where, according to a South Korean biographer, he was addressed as "the premier's son." He went to work in the central committee of the Korean Workers Party, first as a ministerial assistant, swiftly becoming a senior official in the propaganda and agitation department, which controlled much of the party's agenda.

Kim was working his way up the system, and working the system, but also looking over his shoulder. Nothing in his rise to power would be easy or preordained. Dynastic succession was far from inevitable, and even if there was to be a dynasty, it was not clear whether Kim would be its beneficiary. His uncle, Kim Young Ju, was a senior government official. More threatening, however, was Kim's new stepmother: Kim Song Ae, a typist whom Kim Il-sung married in the early 1960's.

According to accounts from defectors, as well as from Chinese and Soviet visitors to North Korea, Kim Jong-il did not get along with his stepmother. There are unconfirmed stories that he tore her face out of pictures. Kim Song Ae became a member of the central committee of the Korean Workers Party, giving her a position from which to influence succession. She had children with Kim Il-sung, and one of their sons, Kim Pyong Il, was viewed as a possible heir because of his intelligence and likeness to his father. (Famously, Kim Jong-il was several inches shorter than his father, an inconvenience that led him to wear platform shoes.)

As he moved to secure his position, Kim needed to remain in the good graces of his father while outmaneuvering his stepmother, half-brother, uncle and anyone else — particularly the country's powerful generals — who wished to lead North Korea.

Kim Il-sung's regime did not take long to veer from Communist orthodoxy and become a personality cult of the sort perfected by Stalin in the Soviet Union. In the early 1970's, North Koreans began wearing lapel pins bearing the likeness of the Great Leader, as the official media described Kim Il-sung; he was portrayed as, basically, infallible. The elite was purged of anyone with wavering loyalty or anyone who might develop wavering loyalties; Kim Il-sung placed close relatives at his side.

During this period, Kim Jong-il was working hard to smooth his way to power.

"I had an impression that he was implementing his plans to get rid of even those very close to Kim Il-sung, including his uncle," Hwang wrote. "In order to show his father that he was the most loyal, he singled out people near Kim Il-sung. Arguing that these people were not loyal and citing doubts about their ideology or competency, he would relentlessly attack and remove them."

Until recently, conventional wisdom held that through the 70's and 80's Kim Jong-il filled his nights with parties and days with terrorism. In 1987, two North Korean agents placed a bomb aboard a Korean Air Lines flight, killing all 115 people on board. One agent, a young woman, was caught and said after extradition to Seoul that her controllers told her the attack was ordered by Kim Jong-il.

Whatever his role in terrorism, it has become clear that Kim Jong-il was running North Korea well before his ailing father died in 1994, at the age of 82, of an apparent heart attack. In the years before his death, according to Hwang, "Kim Il-sung was not the Kim Il-sung of years past. Most of his vitality had disappeared, and he was turning into an old man concerned only with successfully handing over power to Kim Jong-il."

Many North Korea experts believe Kim Jong-il stayed in the background for the sake of appearances: In a Confucian society, a son must defer, publicly, to his father. If Kim Jong-il moved too rashly, he might have engendered resentment from elderly members of the military whose backing or quiescence he needed.

One way he cemented his hold on power was to do as his father did: place close relatives in influential positions. Kim's sister, Kim Kyung Hee, became a powerful figure within the Korean Workers Party and has been referred to in the government media as "First Lady." Her husband, Chang Song Taek, heads the party's organizational department. His brother, Chang Song U, commands the army district that defends Pyongyang.

Kim's control over the military and his insinuation of loyalists into key command positions are a linchpin of his hold on power. He travels often within North Korea, particularly to military bases, because, as he told the South Korean media chiefs, "my power comes from the military." Though he has many posts, including general secretary of the Korean Workers Party, the one that truly counts is his chairmanship of the National Defense Commission, which controls the armed forces.

Kim's regime is best understood as an imperial court, clouded in intrigue, not unlike the royal households that ruled Japan, China and, throughout most of its existence, Korea itself. Until the 20th century, Korea was led by feudal kings, notably the Yi dynasty. By creating a personal and uncaring regime, Kim Il-sung wasn't stealing a page from only Stalin; he was also stealing it from Korean history, a fact that helps explain its durability.

"North Korea is a semifeudal society that is still based on traditional Korean values," says Alexandre Mansourov, a scholar at the Asia Pacific Center for Security Studies who was a Soviet diplomat based in Pyongyang in the 1980's. "There are traces of modernity, but if you look at the structure of thinking, it is very traditional, in a medieval sense."

A hallmark of emperors is lavish court entertainment in the face of poverty or distress in their domains. Kim Jong-il appeared to be cut from this imperial cloth. Through the 70's and 80's, stories emerged from North Korea of wild parties Kim Jong-il held, attended by beautiful women and drunken men. One of the finest accounts of that era comes from Choi Eun Hee, a popular South Korean actress who was kidnapped from Hong Kong in 1978 and bundled off to North Korea. Kim was disappointed with the backward state of North Korea's film industry, so he tried to jump-start it by ordering the kidnapping of Choi and, shortly thereafter, her husband, Shin Sang Ok, a director in Seoul.

After they were taken to Pyongyang, he explained to them, in a conversation that they surreptitiously recorded, "I just said, 'I need those two people, so bring them here,' so my comrades just carried out the operation." Eight years later, after making a number of films in North Korea, Choi and Shin escaped while visiting Vienna.

In a memoir she wrote with her husband, "Kidnapped to the North Korean Paradise," which has not been published in English, Choi recalls being woken one morning at 5 at the guarded villa where Kim had placed her. Her controller told her to get dressed quickly, but wouldn't say why. Within minutes, a Mercedes arrived at the villa and whisked her into central Pyongyang, to a building used for Kim Jong-il's parties.

"As I entered," Choi wrote, "I was assaulted with the pungent odor of alcohol. Farther inside, I saw quite a spectacle. Forty or 50 people apparently had partied all night. The men were drunk, and there were several women I had never seen before."

They perked up when the actress arrived. She was prevailed upon to have a drink, then another and another. The Dear Leader was not in mint condition; his eyes were bloodshot, and his speech was slurred. He had apparently been drinking all night long.

"A band was performing in the front of the room," Choi wrote. "All the girls were in their 20's. Kim Jong-il, drunk, gave a string of requests. Songs changed according to his request. The girls looked tired. He asked me to conduct the band. I declined, but then the others joined in on the request: 'Comrade Choi, our beloved leader doesn't let just anybody conduct the band. It's a great honor. Do it.' "

So she did it. She soon felt ill from the alcohol, and Kim Jong-il ordered one of the women to take her to a room upstairs to rest. She fell asleep on a sofa, but was soon woken by a senior party official. "I felt lips on my cheek," she recalled. She slapped the official and told him to get lost.

Accounts of this sort gave the impression, outside North Korea, that Kim Jong-il was no more competent to take charge of his homeland than Hugh Hefner. Now, however, his bacchanalian ways are being viewed from a different, subtler perspective. As anyone who has spent time with South Korean or Japanese politicians knows, boozing and womanizing are an integral part of their political culture. Your drinking buddy is your political ally. It is the equivalent, in Tokyo and Seoul, of jogging with George W. Bush. Bonds are forged; loyalties, rewarded.

While at high school, Kim Jong-il had a close friend whose older brother was married to a particularly attractive young woman, Sung Hae Rim. At the time she was 19. Kim noticed her beauty, as teenage boys do, but nothing came of it until he graduated from college and, while working at the central committee, immersed himself in a passion that would remain with him for the rest of his life: movies. He often visited Pyongyang's main film studio to watch movies and visit sets. He would later receive credit for producing at least a half dozen films and musicals, and he wrote two books, "On the Art of Cinema" and "Kim Jong-il on the Art of Opera" (both works are sold at Amazon.com).

During one visit to the studio, he again noticed Sung Hae Rim, who had become an actress and was usually cast in the role of a heroine. One thing led to another, and Kim fell in love. Inconveniently, Sung Hae Rim was married and had a child, but according to her sister, Sung Hae Rang, who defected in 1996 and recently published a memoir in Korean, Kim forced Sung to leave her husband and live with him.

It was a strange and tragic situation. Kim could not marry Sung because of her previous marriage, her child and the fact that she was six years his senior; in a Confucian society, a match of that sort would be frowned upon, especially for a man who was to inherit a nation. Kim did not even feel safe telling his strait-laced father about his new love; the affair could bump him off the fast track to succession.

According to Sung Hae Rang's memoir, which is called "Wisteria House," her sister was moved to one of Kim's secluded villas and rarely traveled outside of it. In 1971, she became pregnant. This posed a logistical inconvenience, because Kim could not visit the hospital where she gave birth. To do so would reveal to prying eyes that he was the father of an illegitimate child.

Sung's sister wrote that Kim and Sung arranged a covert system to inform him of his child's birth and its sex. Kim parked his car outside the hospital every night she was there and flicked his lights on and off to signal that it was he. Once the baby was born, Sung signaled back the birth of the child and its sex by flicking the room's light on and off in a prearranged sequence.

The child was a boy, and he was named Kim Jong Nam. Within a few years of his birth, Sung Hae Rim began suffering insomnia and other nervous disorders. She was sent to Moscow for treatment at sanitariums and spent most of the remainder of her life there; she died in Russia in 2002. When her sister left for Moscow, Sung Hae Rang was put in charge of the boy's upbringing. Though it became known in Pyongyang that he was Kim Jong-il's son, Kim Jong Nam remained cloistered at different villas and was eventually sent with Song Hae Rang and her son, Lee Il Nam, to Geneva, where Kim Jong Nam was enrolled at a private school. Lee Il Nam disappeared from Geneva and emerged later in Seoul. He wrote a memoir about his life in the Dear Leader's household, and in 1997 he was killed in what South Korean officials say was an assassination by North Korean agents.

The palace intrigue had other chapters. Kim Il-sung became aware of Kim Jong-il's affair and disapproved of it. In the early 70's, he ordered his son to marry Kim Young Sook, the daughter of a senior military official. Although Kim Jong-il does not spend much time with his "official" wife, she has remained loyal to him. She is not considered a power broker. She bore a daughter by Kim; the daughter has played no role in politics.

Kim soon fell for yet another woman, Ko Young Hee, a dancer who caught his eye when her troupe performed at one of his parties. A delicate beauty, she was from a family of Koreans who had lived in Japan and immigrated to North Korea in the 1960's. Kim could not wed her — he was already married, after all — so he housed her in still another of his villas. She soon bore him two sons, and last year she was spoken of publicly — and favorably — in the North Korean media, suggesting that her sons were rising in official esteem. Early this month, however, a Japanese newspaper reported that Ko Young Hee was seriously injured in a car crash.

In 2001, Kim Jong Nam was detained at Narita airport, outside Tokyo, as he was trying to enter the country with two women and a 4-year-old boy on a fraudulent passport from the Dominican Republic. He said he just wanted to visit Tokyo Disneyland. He was expelled to China. Because, in part, of this embarrassment, Kim Jong Nam is no longer considered a front-runner for succession; two North Korea watchers in Seoul told me that he lives in China and is afraid to return to North Korea. It now appears that Kim Jong Chul, 22, the Dear Leader's son by his mistress Ko Young Hee, is first in line for succession.

At 8 in the morning on July 26, 2001, a five-car train rolled into Khasan, which is on the Russian side of the border between Russia and North Korea. A carpeted platform was brought to the main car, and when its door opened, Kim Jong-il emerged, waving and smiling to the officials assembled at the station. Kim was embarking on the longest foreign trip in his adult life, a 24-day rail odyssey across Russia.

Journalists scrambled to various cities on the itinerary — Khabarovsk, Omsk, St. Petersburg and Moscow — hoping to catch a glimpse of the mysterious North Korean. Few of them succeeded, because Kim was kept far apart from inquiring eyes. He traveled in an armored rail car, with a locomotive seven minutes ahead to make sure the track was safe and another locomotive several minutes behind to make sure nobody could commandeer a train and ram it into the rear of the Dear Leader's caravan.

For the Russians who escorted Kim, the trip offered the first prolonged encounter foreigners would have with him. The informal silence about the trip lasted for more than a year, until Konstantin Pulikovsky, a presidential envoy who headed the Russian delegation escorting Kim, published a memoir in Russian about the journey. This led other officials to discuss it, including Georgy Toloraya, a diplomat who had been based in North Korea and speaks fluent Korean.

The Dear Leader, it turns out, does not travel third class. His train was stocked with live lobster, French wine and fresh pastries, and his entourage included four young women who entertained him and his companions by singing songs in Korean and Russian. One car was a meeting room with two flat-panel screens, one for films (videos of military parades were among his favorites) and the other for a satellite-updated map of the train's progress, much like the ones in airplane cabins.

Kim visited an array of sites, including a pig farm, a brewery, a space firm and the Hermitage Museum. He even went to a department store in Khabarovsk, where he stopped at the perfume department and asked where the scents came from. He spent a few minutes in the beauty salon and also visited the sports department, where skis and sportswear were sold; he rubbed the fabrics to assess their quality. In the men's-wear department, he inquired why some pants had cuffs and some didn't, and he seemed surprised at the cost of Italian shoes — about $400.

"Do people here really buy such expensive shoes?" he asked.

For the Russians, Kim's rail odyssey confirmed what they had been thinking of the Dear Leader — that he is smart and wants to reform his country's failed economy, but does not wish to lose power. "When I read somewhere that he is a madman who doesn't understand what he is doing — that is laughable stuff," said Toloraya, the Russian diplomat who was on the train and met Kim on several dozen occasions. Toloraya is now the Russian consul general in Sydney, and I interviewed him on the phone. "He is a professional in state governance. What he does is very well prepared. It would be a mistake to think of him as an impossible, unpredictable character. He is an emotional person, but he is a professional. He knows what he is doing. He plans several steps ahead."

The Russians weren't the only ones getting to know the charms and wishes of the Dear Leader. Kim's coming-out to the rest of the world included, in October 2000, an unprecedented visit to North Korea by an American delegation led by Secretary of State Albright. This was in the waning days of the Clinton administration, before the 1994 nuclear agreement fell apart, and Albright wanted to sound out Kim on a plan for ending his missile-production program; Kim, in return, wanted Clinton to visit Pyongyang.

The Americans were in for some surprises.

The North Koreans had promised that Albright would see Kim, but when she arrived in Pyongyang, her schedule did not include a meeting with him. Her delegation was whisked into the city in the early morning, to the guest house where they would stay, and shortly afterward they were taken on a tour that many foreign visitors go through in Pyongyang, highlighted — that may not be the right word — by a visit to the tomb of Kim Il-sung.

At lunch, Albright was abruptly told she would meet Kim in the afternoon. The delegation was driven to his guest house, and as Albright stood in front of a huge mural depicting a storm at sea, Kim walked in, greeting her with both hands extended forward. They were about the same height, Albright in her heels and Kim in his platform shoes.

He poured on the charm. Kim asked Albright if she had seen any recent films, and when she replied "Gladiator," Kim said he had seen "Amistad," which he described as "very sad." He proudly told Wendy Sherman, who was in Pyongyang as special adviser to Clinton on North Korea: "I own all the Academy Award movies. I've watched them all."

Smart as he is, Kim lives in a different world and doesn't always realize it. One evening, the Albright delegation was shepherded into a stadium in Pyongyang, where they were seated next to Kim. For the next two hours the Americans were treated to a "mass game" — a fantasia of synchronized gymnastics on the stadium floor and card-turning displays on the opposite side of the stadium. The exactitude of these "games" is terrifying. They are often staged on important national occasions; dignitaries from friendly countries were invited to a particularly spectacular display to mark Kim Jong-il's birthday last year. I attended a mass game display in Pyongyang in 1989, and the sensation a Westerner feels is not artistic appreciation but totalitarian horror.

One card montage performed for Albright showed a North Korean missile being launched into the sky. It was an odd display for Americans who were negotiating a cessation of missile production and research. But Kim, ever the showman, turned to Albright on his right and said, "That was our first missile launch and our last." To make sure his message got through, he turned to Sherman on his left and repeated his statement. The meaning was clear: the missile program can be stopped if you offer us a new relationship. "This was totally orchestrated, the cards and turning to us," Sherman said when I spoke with her at the Washington office of the Albright Group, a consulting firm. "For all I know, that was the purpose of taking us to the stadium."

Albright and Sherman returned to Washington convinced that Kim Jong-il's stated intentions should be put to the test: he should be offered a new relationship with the U.S. government, including a visit by Clinton to North Korea, if he was willing to submit to a verifiable agreement on halting missile research, production, deployment and exports. This was a position that critics would certainly attack as appeasement, but for Albright and Sherman, it was a price worth paying to end the North Korean missile threat.

"I have no illusions about Kim," Sherman said. "He's charming but totally controlling. He is a leader who has left his people with no freedom, no choices, no food, no future. People are executed. There are labor camps. But the decision we have to make is whether to try to deal with him to open the country so that the people of North Korea do have freedom, do have choices, do have food. Do I think it would be preferable to not deal with him? Yes, but the consequences are horrible, so you have to deal with him."

The clock ran out. There wasn't enough time before Clinton left office to negotiate the agreements that would need to be in place before Air Force One could take off for North Korea. The momentum halted with the advent of the Bush administration. But now, with the second round of six-party talks nearing, the Americans are trying to figure out once again whether and how to deal with Kim.

Choe Hak Rae, the former newspaper publisher, remains hopeful. The way he sees it, Kim Jong-il knows his economy has failed and wants to reform it. Signs of change in the north are already evident: some prices have been deregulated, farmers' markets have been established and North Korean officials have been dispatched to foreign countries to learn about business. The bear wants to get out of its cage, Choe says. "The more he is regarded as the worst person of the century, the more he will become a dangerous man," Choe told me. "But if safety and security are guaranteed for himself and North Korea, I don't think he will be a danger."

Wendy Sherman is more cautious, but she and other advocates of engagement say that Kim believes, erroneously, that he can control the tempo and impact of opening up to the rest of the world. It is not clear yet whether her point of view has much traction in the Bush administration, which veers from warlike hostility to occasional murmurs of peaceful coexistence if Kim disarms.

The notion that a dictator like Kim can be coaxed to reform has no real historical precedent. The most notable totalitarian regimes of the modern era — the ones developed by Stalin in the Soviet Union and by Mao Zedong in China — were not reformed by the men who shaped them. Reform of such states requires a degree of repudiation that the authors of failure are loath to tolerate, mostly out of fear for their own survival. In essence, proponents of engagement hope Kim will begin a process that will lead to his downfall. It seems doubtful that he will be sufficiently selfless or stupid to do that.

The disarmament question is even stickier. The administration has waged two pre-emptive wars on countries it deemed to be enemies — Afghanistan and Iraq. It does not require Kissingerian smarts to calculate that a member of the axis of evil would be death-wish foolish to relinquish the weapons of mass destruction that may be the only thing, by virtue of the horrible implications of their use, that stands in the way of an American attack. The real issue isn't whether Kim is crazy enough to amass a nuclear arsenal but whether he is crazy enough to dispossess himself of his one bargaining chip.

What is the solution? I decided to seek out a man who knows Kim Jong-il better than anyone else outside North Korea: Hwang Jang Yop. Hwang was the Karl Rove of North Korea for more than three decades, creating the ideology of Juche, or self-sufficiency, that was the bedrock of Kim Il-sung's regime and remains in place today — though in name only, since North Korea depends on foreign aid for its survival. Working at the center of the regime, Hwang learned what Kim Jong-il wants, what he can do and what he will not do.

On a Saturday morning in August, I went with my interpreter to a private club in Seoul, where I met Cho Gab Je, a prominent conservative journalist who edits a magazine, the Monthly Chosun, that is known for its hard-hitting coverage of North Korea. We got into a sedan and drove to an office building in a suburb of the city; Cho is friendly with Hwang and arranged for me to meet him. I agreed to not provide details of the building or its location, other than to say that the anteroom is guarded by a number of armed security agents and that you must pass through a metal detector before entering Hwang's office. Hwang's caution is understandable: North Korea is believed to have agents in the South who would be eager to silence their homeland's most famous traitor.

Hwang is 80 and hard of hearing; I sat in an armchair to his immediate left. He is small and thin and was dressed in a dark blue suit and blue tie. He is not particularly warm with visitors or, it would seem, with anybody. Though he lived a privileged life in North Korea — he had a phone at his home, ample food and a car, and he traveled extensively outside the country — his defection has brought doom onto his family. His wife is rumored to have committed suicide after his defection, as did his daughter, who is said to have jumped out of a bus that was taking her to a prison camp. It is assumed that his other children and grandchildren are in prison camps, if they are still alive.

He does not talk about his personal life, but he does talk about the Dear Leader.

"If I were to go into details, it would take many days," he said. "As a politician or leader who can work for the development of the state and the happiness of the people, he is an F student, a dropout. But as a dictator he has an excellent ability. He can organize people so that they can't move, can't do anything, and he can keep them under his ideology. As far as I know, the present North Korean dictatorial system is the most precise and thorough in history."

Hwang says that he believes foreign aid has helped Kim by providing the resources he needs to retain the loyalty of his core constituencies — the military and party elites. Hwang says he does not believe Kim would ever allow foreign aid and investment to benefit the people who need it; Kim has shown no interest in his people's material well-being, and given the choice between regime survival and national prosperity, it's pretty clear which he would prefer. A few years ago, Kim began letting South Koreans visit the north, and this was seen as a relaxation of the isolation of his information-starved subjects. But the tourists, whose visits provide much-needed hard currency to the regime, are shepherded in quarantinelike conditions that make them virtual prisoners; contact with ordinary North Koreans is nil. Hwang says outsiders are naïve to believe that Kim is ready to open up his country.

"South Korea is being fooled, and the Chinese, who should know best," he said. "A considerable number of people are being fooled, including the United States."

Hwang's synopsis of Kim's dictatorship reminded me of a passage from his memoir. He wrote about a 1992 banquet that Kim presided over in Pyongyang; a dance troupe provided lavishly choreographed entertainment.

The performance "was enough to elicit disgust when seen through the eyes of people with healthy minds," Hwang wrote, recalling that he nonetheless applauded vigorously for the entertainers. A professor who was next to him was flummoxed.

"Are you clapping because you really enjoy the performance?" the professor asked.

"It doesn't matter," Hwang replied. "Just clap like mad. It's an order."

Kim's hold on power depends not only on his willingness to impose misery upon his people but also on the willingness of the North Korean elite to accept their privileges and say nothing. Many North Koreans are well aware of the repressed and backward state of their homeland and wish it were otherwise; recent visitors say North Koreans quietly express a desire for greater contact with the outside world. The problem is that none of them are prepared to force or even nudge their wishes upon Kim Jong-il. The Dear Leader understands, as smart tyrants do, that perpetual clapping is generated by terror. That is why he works 20 hours a day to make sure the applause of fear does not stop.

When his regime is brought to an end, as one day it will be, the cause will not be his napping. Kim has had plenty of time, and he has worked hard, to insulate himself from the type of events that have led to the collapse of other tyrannies and dynasties. But the downfall of dictators is unpredictable. The collapse of the Soviet Union, the dissolution of its Eastern European brethren, the easing of Maoist discipline in China — these happened in ways that were not foreseen. It is very likely, too, that the unimaginable will get Kim Jong-il in the end.

IN LOCKSTEP

In June 2002, the Japanese photographer Koichiro Otaki was given a rare opportunity to photograph the "mass games," choreographed performances that were held to celebrate the 60th birthday of Kim Jong-il. The games, held in the gigantic May Day Stadium in Pyongyang, involved more than 100,000 participants, mostly students; they took place six days a week for two months. Dancers on the field performed elaborate and precisely coordinated routines, while people in the stands held up intricate sequences of colored cards to create huge mosaic-like images.

Korean Leaders Meet in Pyongyang

BY CHOE SANG-HUN | OCT. 2, 2007

SEOUL, SOUTH KOREA, OCT. 2 — Stepping into the international spotlight at a delicate time for his isolated regime, the reclusive North Korean leader, Kim Jong-il, welcomed President Roh Moo-hyun of South Korea to Pyongyang today for three days of talks.

It was only the second meeting between leaders of the two Koreas since the country was divided 60 years ago, and Mr. Kim had mobilized a huge crowd to welcome Mr. Roh, who came with offers of peace and economic aid.

The North Korean leader himself was dour and reserved, however, in contrast to his effusive manner in 2000, during the first such meeting. Then, broadly smiling, he had hugged Kim Dae-jung, the South Korean president, a scene that softened his image in South Korea and beyond.

This morning, Pyongyang's usually drab sidewalks blossomed in color as North Koreans dressed in their holiday best waved pink and red paper flowers, according to South Korean television images from Pyongyang. Hundreds of thousands of spectators erupted into well-choreographed chants of "hooray" and "unify the fatherland" as Mr. Roh rode through central Pyongyang in an open limousine with Kim Yong-nam, who is the North's nominal head of state but ranks second to Mr. Kim in power. The two held talks later in the day.

Formal talks with Kim Jong-il begin Wednesday.

Mr. Roh travels with a bold initiative: If North Korea agrees to work toward reducing a half century of animosity with arms cuts, the South will help rebuild the North's moribund economy, creating a "joint economic community" as a prelude to eventual reunification.

Mr. Roh will also test Mr. Kim's willingness to give up his nuclear arsenal in return for economic rewards and diplomatic relations with the United States and other countries. Mr. Roh's aides believe that the summit meeting, together with recent progress in six-nation talks on

POOL/GETTY IMAGES

Kim Jong-il (left) meets with South Korean President Roh Moo-hyun on October 2, 2007.

North Korea's nuclear disarmament, is a sign that the North is cautiously embracing more cooperation and reform. But some analysts warn that the meeting may also be another tactical move by Mr. Kim to obtain more economic concessions without giving up nuclear weapons.

Mr. Kim, 65, was unsmiling as the two leaders exchanged a businesslike handshake and a terse "Nice to meet you" in front of a cultural hall in Pyongyang, where Mr. Roh's motorcade stopped for a welcoming ceremony. Clad in his trademark khaki tunic, Mr. Kim walked down a red carpet, guiding the South Korean leader past a parade of North Korean soldiers goose-stepping with bayonet-tipped rifles.

Appearing before a live international audience, the pudgy Mr. Kim dispelled recent news reports that he was so sick that he could hardly walk. Besides an expected aid package, Mr. Roh's visit brings a propaganda bonus to the Kim government, which cannot feed its people without foreign aid but boasts that its nuclear arsenal compels respect from the rest of the world.

The North's state propagandists have described visits by foreign leaders, including former President Jimmy Carter in 1994 and Secretary of State Madeleine Albright in 2000, as paying tribute to their "Great Leader."

In his journey to Pyongyang early today, Mr. Roh drove three and a half hours from Seoul, the South Korean capital. He was accompanied by industry leaders, politicians, cultural figures and scholars.

About 30 miles north of Seoul, Mr. Roh stepped out of his vehicle to make the symbolic gesture of walking across the border that divides the Koreas. He was the first South Korean leader to cross it on foot. In 2000, Kim Dae-jung flew to Pyongyang.

"This line is a wall that has divided the nation for a half-century," Mr. Roh said, as he stepped across a yellow strip with the words "peace and prosperity" written on it. Our people have suffered from too many hardships, and development has been held up due to this wall. This line will be gradually erased and the wall will fall."

Before leaving Seoul, Mr. Roh said he would strive for "substantive and concrete progress that will bring about a peace settlement together with economic development."

The two Koreas remain technically at war since the 1950-53 Korean War ended in a cease-fire, and that status is considered by many South Koreans as a root cause of tension on the divided peninsula.

Mr. Roh said he would use his visit to help make progress in six-nation talks, where regional powers have been trying for years to end the North's nuclear weapons programs. United States officials warn that any attempt to replace the Korean armistice with a formal peace treaty — a process that would involve the United States and China, both parties to the Korean War — must be preceded by progress in nuclear talks.

"I certainly am not looking for those inter-Korean discussions to change the basic facts on the ground or the six-party talks," Tom Casey, the State Department spokesman, said Monday.

This week's summit meeting comes almost exactly a year after the North tested a nuclear bomb, rattling regional stability and persuading the Bush administration to abandon its earlier policy of not engaging a government it had earlier vilified as part of the "axis of evil." Since then, North Korea has shut down its nuclear reactor, its main source of weapons-grade plutonium, and has tentatively agreed to disable its nuclear facilities by the end of the year.

But the North Koreans have not firmly committed themselves to the more difficult aspects of denuclearization: providing full details of their programs, dismantling their programs and giving up actual stores of fissile material and weapons.

Despite widely voiced doubts over what the talks this week can accomplish, the South Korean government insists that a face-to-face meeting with Mr. Kim, whose words carry ultimate authority, can help clarify the North's intentions.

"Kim Jong-il must make a strategic decision. How long is the North going to beg rice, fertilizer and other aid from the international community?" said Lee Su-hoon, chairman of Seoul's Presidential Committee on Northeast Cooperation Initiative, before he accompanied Roh to Pyongyang. "Kim Jong-il must seize this opportunity."

By appearing more forthcoming, analysts in South Korea say, Mr. Kim can encourage a new movement in Washington to engage his Communist government and make it easier for South Korea and China to continue providing financial support. But if Mr. Roh promises economic aid without winning tangible concessions, he may stoke criticism that unilateral aid only shores up Mr. Kim's repressive system.

Conservative political opposition in Seoul have called the trip a gambit by Mr. Roh to create a "unification euphoria" to help sway votes in the presidential election set for this December. Mr. Roh is barred by running again for president, but opinion surveys show that liberal candidates favored by him are lagging far behind the main opposition candidate, Lee Myung-bak.

North Korea Tries to Show Its Leader Is Healthy and in Control

BY CHOE SANG-HUN | NOV. 6, 2008

SEOUL, SOUTH KOREA — North Korea's state-run media outlets have released a flurry of reports of public appearances by the North's reclusive leader, Kim Jong-il, in what analysts on Thursday described as an effort to demonstrate to his people and the outside world that he is firmly in control, despite widespread rumors of ill health.

Since Sunday, news outlets in the North have described three separate appearances by Mr. Kim, 66, who officials in Washington and Seoul have said probably suffered a stroke around August and may have undergone brain surgery.

In the latest such report, the North's official news agency, KCNA, said on Thursday that Mr. Kim had attended a concert, where a state choir and opera groups performed numbers like "Please Receive Our Salute!"

Photographs of Mr. Kim that have accompanied these reports have been studied by North Korea watchers in government and media. Aided by neurosurgeons and other experts, they have scrutinized every detail, from Mr. Kim's facial expressions to background scenery, to gauge his condition.

"The reports and release of his pictures are carefully calculated and timed," said Ryoo Kihl-jae, a professor at the University of North Korean Studies in Seoul. "It's Kim Jong-il's way of responding to the intense outside attention to him. He is a man very sensitive to how the outside world views him."

But the photographs have raised as many questions as they have answered. North Korea's state media did not say when the pictures were taken, confounding the analysts.

Undated pictures released on Oct. 11, for example, showed Mr. Kim inspecting a military unit and looking healthy. But they showed green foliage, while trees on the Korean Peninsula at the time were tinged with red and gold.

Then, on Sunday, North Korea issued two photos of Mr. Kim, saying he was watching a soccer match. This time, the background vegetation had appropriately autumnal colors.

In one picture, he was smiling. The smile, experts said, was symmetrical enough to exclude any serious paralysis of the facial muscles, a common occurrence among people who suffered a stroke.

Mr. Kim also had a full head of hair, despite reports that he might have had a brain surgery.

But the experts also noted that in both pictures Mr. Kim's left hand looked immobile, either resting limply on his lap or in a pocket. They also noted that he was not wearing the shoes he usually uses to elevate his short stature.

Such details led news media to speculate that Mr. Kim might be suffering paralysis on the left side of his body.

On Wednesday, 14 photographs were released that seemed intended to dispel such notions. They showed Mr. Kim walking about and clapping his hands.

"The fact that the North is going to such lengths to demonstrate that Kim Jong-il is O.K. is, ironically, a sign that his health is not normal," Mr. Ryoo said.

Other analysts said the timing of recent reports about Mr. Kim was linked to the American presidential election.

"Kim Jong-il wants to show that he is in control and that he has no problem being a partner of dialogue with the United States," said Kim Yong-yun, a North Korea expert at Dongguk University.

He suggested that the North Korean leader might soon stage a "foolproof" demonstration of his health, for example by releasing a video of his public activities or paying a courtesy call to the Chinese Embassy in the North Korean capital, Pyongyang. China is North Korea's main ally.

North Korea Takes Steps to Extend Dynastic Rule

BY CHOE SANG-HUN | SEPT. 2, 2010

SEOUL, SOUTH KOREA — Kim Jong-il, the North Korean leader, is expected to convene a rare congress of the ruling Workers' Party in coming days to pave the way for his son to succeed him, a feat of political engineering that would be a first in the Communist world: extending dynastic rule to a third generation.

Ahead of the national congress, the first ceremonial conclave of the party's delegates in decades, Mr. Kim's propaganda machine is busily reminding North Koreans that their nation owes it existence to Mr. Kim's father, Kim Il-sung, who was a leader of anti-Japanese guerrillas in Manchuria in the early 20th century.

The meeting, like all political events in the North, will be secret, and even the precise starting date has not been publicly confirmed. North Korea has said that the party's "highest leading body" will be elected at the meeting; beyond that, the agenda is unknown, and it is unclear how the expected promotion of Mr. Kim's third son, Kim Jong-un, will be presented. But Mr. Kim's recent trip to China, North Korea's main patron and supporter, which followed the announcement of the meeting, has fueled speculation that a momentous transition is under way.

"This party meeting will be a coming-out party for Kim Jong-un," said Peter Beck, a North Korea expert at Keio University in Japan.

Little is known about the son, believed to be in his late 20s, and no photos or public sightings of him have been reported since he attended a Swiss school as a teenager. After his father's stroke in 2008, however, his grooming as heir picked up speed. He has accompanied Mr. Kim on visits to factories and military units and is getting policy briefings, according to South Korean intelligence officials who monitor developments in the North.

Songs, poems and posters alluding to the son are in circulation, they say. North Korean media have not mentioned the son by name, but propaganda has hinted about the virtues of transferring power to a younger generation. Kim Jong-il, who took over when his father died in 1994, began building his "military first" leadership platform 50 years ago as a teenager, official media say.

Under Mr. Kim's military-oriented rule, the Workers' Party has withered. The last time the party held its congress, a 1980 meeting during which Mr. Kim sealed his position as successor by assuming crucial party posts, the party's Politburo had 34 members. Now it has only eight, as those who have died have not been replaced.

"A new force will come in who will pave the way for the succession and support the young, inexperienced kid as leader," said Chang Yong-seok, research director at the Institute for Peace Affairs in Seoul. "If a new generation of leaders comes in, this is not a bad thing. They could be less bound by ideology and more pragmatic about opening up."

Historically, the Kim family has used party caucuses to purge political enemies, as well as proclaim long-term visions for the country. Recently, there has been an unusually large number of reports about top-ranking North Korean officials being executed, killed in mysterious traffic accidents or declared missing.

Jang Song-taek, Mr. Kim's brother-in-law, and hard-line generals on Mr. Kim's National Defense Commission, the country's top ruling body, are expected to move into crucial party posts to ensure a smooth transition of power, analysts say. Less clear is whether Mr. Kim is confident enough to place his son in the Politburo and the party's Central Military Commission.

Woo Seong-ji, a professor at Kyung Hee University in Seoul, said that he believed Mr. Kim might start his son in a rather modest post to "lessen the shock" and buy time to build his leadership credentials.

Mr. Beck of Keio University said: "He can't be too prominent because he is not known to the North Korean public. They have to make the sale to the public. But they have to make the sale to some of the elite, too."

It is unclear what other changes might be on the agenda.

During his meeting with Mr. Kim in Changchun, in northeastern China, last Friday, President Hu Jintao urged North Korea to follow China's example by adopting a "market mechanism," according to Chinese media. Mr. Kim toured factories and expressed interest in how China had sought to reinvigorate a region just across the North Korean border.

Faced with international sanctions, Mr. Kim may view stronger economic ties with China as one blueprint he can offer at the party congress, said Jin Jingyi, a North Korea expert at Peking University.

The North Korean government survived the first health scare set off by Mr. Kim's stroke without much instability. That showed that Mr. Kim's inner circle, whose political fortunes rest with the Kim family's dynastic rule, would be likely to ensure a smooth transfer of power to the son even if Mr. Kim suddenly died, analysts said.

"I think he is chosen exactly because he is young," said Andrei Lankov, a North Korea expert at Kookmin University in Seoul. "In case of his father's sudden death, Kim Jong-un — inexperienced, without power base, embarrassingly young — will have no choice but to obediently follow the instructions of the old guard. He will be a dictator, but merely a rubber-stamping dictator. This is what the people in the position of power want."

Kim Jong-il, Dictator Who Turned North Korea Into a Nuclear State, Dies

BY DAVID E. SANGER | DEC. 18, 2011

CALLED THE "DEAR LEADER" by his people, Kim Jong-il presided with an iron hand over a country he kept on the edge of starvation and collapse, fostering perhaps the last personality cult in the Communist world even as he banished citizens deemed disloyal to gulags or sent assassins after defectors.

He came to power after the death in 1994 of his father, Kim Il-sung, North Korea's founder. His inheritance was an impoverished country with an uncertain place in a post-cold-war era. He played his one card, his nuclear weapons program, brilliantly, first defying efforts by the administration of George W. Bush to push his country over the brink, then exploiting America's distraction with the war in Iraq to harvest enough nuclear fuel from his main nuclear reactor at Yongbyon to produce the fuel for six to eight weapons.

Throughout, he remained an unknowable figure. Everything about him was guesswork, from the exact date and place of his birth to the mythologized events of his rise in a country formed by the hasty division of the Korean Peninsula at the end of World War II.

North Koreans heard about him only as their "peerless leader" and "the great successor to the revolutionary cause." His portrait hangs beside that of his father, Kim Il-sung, in every North Korean household and building. Towers, banners and even rock faces across the country bear slogans praising him.

Mr. Kim was a source of fascination inside the Central Intelligence Agency, which interviewed his mistresses, tried to track his whereabouts and psychoanalyzed his motives. And he was an object of parody in American culture.

Short and round, he wore elevator shoes, oversize sunglasses and a bouffant hairdo — a Hollywood stereotype of the wacky post-cold-war dictator. Mr. Kim himself was fascinated by film. He orchestrated the kidnapping of an actress and a director, both of them South Koreans, in an effort to build a domestic movie industry. He was said to keep a personal library of 20,000 foreign films, including the complete James Bond series, his favorite. But he rarely saw the outside world, save from the windows of his luxury train, which occasionally took him to China.

He was derided and denounced. President George W. Bush called him a "pygmy" and included his country in the "axis of evil." Children's books in South Korea depicted him as a red devil with horns and fangs. Yet those who met him were surprised by his serious demeanor and his knowledge of events beyond the hermit kingdom he controlled.

"He was a very outspoken person," said Roh Moo-hyun, who as South Korea's president met Mr. Kim in Pyongyang in 2007. "He was the most flexible man in North Korea."

Wendy Sherman, now the No. 3 official in the State Department, who served as counselor to Secretary of State Madeleine K. Albright and accompanied her to North Korea, said in 2008: "He was smart, engaged, knowledgeable, self-confident, sort of the master-director of all he surveyed."

Ms. Albright met Mr. Kim in October 2000 in what turned out to be a futile effort to strike a deal with North Korea over limiting its missile program before President Bill Clinton left office.

"There was no denying the dictatorial state that he ruled," Ms. Sherman said. "There was no denying the freedoms that didn't exist. But at the time, there were a lot of questions in the U.S. about whether he was really in control, and we left with no doubt that he was."

When Ms. Albright and Ms. Sherman sat down to talk through a 14-point list of concerns about North Korea's missile program, "he didn't know the answers to every question, but he knew a lot more than most leaders would — and he was a conceptual thinker," Ms. Sherman added.

A DEAL WITH WASHINGTON

President Bush said during his first term in office that he would never tolerate a nuclear North Korea, but as his presidency wound down, many of his aides believed he did exactly that.

It was not until the spring of 2007 that Mr. Bush was told by the Israelis that North Korea was helping Syria build a nuclear reactor; before the Syrians or the North Koreans were confronted with that evidence, Israel sent bombers on a secret mission to destroy the Syrian plant. The North Koreans have never explained their role.

By the time Mr. Bush left office, the administration had moved from four years of confrontation with the North to three years of halting negotiations. Led by Christopher R. Hill, a veteran American diplomat, the negotiations resulted in a deal that hawks hated: the United States agreed to supply North Korea with large amounts of fuel oil in return for the dismantlement of the aging Yongbyon plant, described by inspectors as a radioactive accident waiting to happen.

Mr. Kim played a weak hand very well. He succeeded in fending off pressure from Washington and Beijing, and forcing Washington to talk with him and ultimately to haggle with him. He chopped up and dragged out negotiations, holding on to his nuclear fuel and whatever weapons he had produced, giving him continued leverage. It is that arsenal that now worries American and Asian officials, who fear that plotting generals and party leaders may fight to control it as they pick Mr. Kim's successor.

"When the history of this era is written," said Graham Allison, a Harvard professor and expert on proliferation, "the scorecard will be Kim 8, Bush 0."

But if "he was the greatest master of survival, against all odds," said Andrei Lankov, a North Korea expert at Kookmin University in Seoul, "it was his own people who paid the price, and the price was pretty high."

Mr. Kim's policy of songun, or "army first," lavished the country's scarce resources on the military, at 1.1 million-strong the world's fifth largest. During his rule, the North expanded its ballistic missile arsenal and, in October 2006, became the eighth country in the world to conduct a nuclear test.

But as the North's economy shrank, its isolation deepened. Possibly as many as 2 million people — almost 10 percent of the population — died in a famine in the mid-to-late 1990s brought on by incompetence and natural disasters.

"Do not expect me to change!" is a popular catchphrase credited to Mr. Kim and used to exhort his people to remain loyal to his socialist ways.

Mr. Kim is believed to have been born in Siberia in 1941, when his father, Kim Il-sung, was in exile in the Soviet Union. But in North Korea's official accounts, he was born in 1942, in a cabin, Abe Lincoln-like. The cabin was in a secret camp of anti-Japanese guerrillas his father commanded on Mount Paektu, a holy piece of land in Korean mythology. The event, the official Korean Central News Agency would often say, was accompanied by the appearance of a bright star in the sky and a double-rainbow that touched the earth.

Little is known of his upbringing, apart from the official statement that he graduated in 1964 from Kim Il-sung University, one of the country's many monuments to his father. At the time, North Korea was enmeshed in the cold war, and the younger Kim watched many crises unfold from close up, including North Korea's seizure of the Pueblo, an American spy ship, in 1968. He appeared episodically at state events, rarely speaking. When he did, he revealed a high-pitched voice and little of his father's easygoing charisma.

In his youth and middle age, there were stories about his playboy lifestyle. There were tales of lavish meals at a time his country was starving — his cook wrote a book after leaving the country — and his wavy hair and lifted heels, along with a passion for top-label liquor, made him the butt of jokes.

There was also speculation that he was involved in the 1983 bombing of a South Korean political delegation in Burma, and that he had known of, and perhaps had ordered, the kidnapping of Japanese citizens. Nothing was proved.

Washington put North Korea on its list of state sponsors of terrorism after North Korean agents planted a bomb that blew up a South Korean passenger jet in 1987 — under instructions from Mr. Kim, according to one of the agents, who was caught alive.

Mr. Kim campaigned for power relentlessly. He bowed to his father at the front porch each morning and offered to put the shoes on the father's feet long before he was elected to the Politburo, at age 32, in 1974, according to a 2006 memoir by Hwang Jang-yop, a former North Korean Workers' Party secretary who was a key aide for the Kim regime before his defection to Seoul in 1997. (Mr. Hwang died in 2010.)

"At an early age, Kim Jong-il mastered the mechanics of power," Mr. Hwang wrote in the memoir.

It was not until 1993, as the existence of the Yongbyon nuclear plant and North Korea's nuclear weapons ambitions became publicly known, that Mr. Kim appeared to be his father's undisputed successor. That year, he became head of the National Defense Commission, the North's most powerful agency, in charge of the military.

In 1994, in a showdown with the United States, North Korea threatened to turn its stockpile of nuclear fuel into bombs. It was the closest the two countries came to war since the armistice that ended the Korean War in 1953. The standoff was defused when Kim Il-sung welcomed former President Jimmy Carter, who pushed Mr. Clinton and Mr. Kim into a deal.

Within a month, however, the country's founder and Great Leader was dead. Many doubted at the time that the younger Kim would take over. There were rumors of a military coup, and theories that he would be allowed to keep his fast cars and to consort with visiting European "entertainers" as long as he did not try to run the country. Like much intelligence about North Korea, that turned out to be wrong.

Mr. Kim has three sons, any of whom could potentially have succeeded him. But his home life is a mystery.

His oldest son, Kim Jong-nam, would have been the natural choice to succeed him. But he had a handicap: his mother never married Mr. Kim. Since his health crisis, in 2008, Mr. Kim had been grooming his third son, Kim Jong-un, believed to be in his late 20s, to be his successor. Reports from North Korea on Monday suggested that Kim Jong-un was in charge.

Mr. Kim consolidated power in the late 1990s, and flexed his muscle by testing a North Korean missile over Japan, sending that much larger and more powerful nation into a panic. It was through episodes like this that Mr. Kim learned true power: that he could blackmail his way to survival.

But he could not learn to feed his own people, and his country became even more dependent on China for food and fuel and on "humanitarian" donations from South Korea and the United States. In June 2000, Mr. Kim played host in Pyongyang, the North's capital, to the first summit meeting with a South Korean president, Kim Dae-jung, since the peninsula was divided more than five decades before.

PRESSURING PYONGYANG

The South Korean leader received the Nobel Peace Prize later that year, though his reputation was soon tainted by revelations that a South Korean company had paid off the North Koreans, and presumably their leader, to arrange the trip.

Once President Bush took office in January 2001, all cooperation between Washington and Seoul over how to deal with the North came to a crashing halt. Mr. Bush rejected the South's "sunshine policy" of engagement with North Korea, and ended Clinton-era talks that he viewed as dangerous appeasement.

A concerted effort began to push North Korea over the brink, and set off an uprising against Kim Jong-il's leadership. To the degree Washington could, it cut off North Korean trade, its access to cash and its ability to export weapons and drugs. Mr. Bush called Mr. Kim a "tyrant" who "starves his own people."

In October 2002, the administration presented North Korea with evidence that it had secretly tried to evade the 1994 nuclear agreement with the United States by purchasing equipment to enrich uranium from Abdul Qadeer Khan, a founder of Pakistan's nuclear weapons program. The evidence was strong — the United States had tracked the shipments with spy satellites — but the C.I.A. overstated its confidence that the North was building separate, secret nuclear facilities.

That led to a confrontation that changed the nature of the North Korean threat. Mr. Kim ordered the ouster of United Nations inspectors who had been stationed at Yongbyon. The United States pressed for an end to fuel shipments to the North. In retaliation, from January through March 2003, just as the United States military was barreling toward the invasion of Iraq, Mr. Kim did what his father had come so very close to doing nine years before: he announced that he was reprocessing spent fuel rods into bomb fuel.

After the invasion of Iraq, Mr. Kim was not seen for nearly two months; there were reports that he had gone into hiding, thinking he was Mr. Bush's next target. He emerged only to start another confrontation in 2006, first with a series of missile tests, then, in October, the North's first nuclear test.

Some Asian and American officials interpreted Mr. Kim's decision as a fit of pique because "six-party talks" — negotiations among North Korea, China, South Korea, Russia, the United States and Japan — were moving so slowly. Others said that Mr. Kim had simply learned from Saddam Hussein's mistakes and determined that he would never face the United States without a nuclear weapon.

The test itself was something of a fizzle; it ended with a sub-kiloton explosion, less than a tenth of the power of the bomb the United States dropped on Hiroshima in 1945. But Mr. Kim had made his point. He was condemned in the United Nations, and China briefly cut off oil and other trade. But within months the United States agreed on a new series of negotiations.

While there were many starts and stops, and disagreements over what it means to fully dismantle a nuclear program, in the summer of 2007 Mr. Kim agreed to stop the production of new nuclear fuel at Yongbyon. By then he presumably had all the weapons he needed.

The plant began to be dismantled, and in the summer of 2008 the Bush administration talked about starting up with Mr. Kim on the hardest negotiations of all, over the price of giving up North Korea's nuclear arsenal. He died before the talks could seriously begin.

As soon as President Obama came into office, Mr. Kim ordered a second nuclear test, this one more successful than the first. And he waited out the predictable hail of international condemnation. The move aborted efforts by Mr. Obama to engage with the North Koreans. And the next three years were spent with the United States and South Korea demanding the North live up to the denuclearization pledges it made during the Bush administration.

Instead, it did the opposite. In November 2010, the North Koreans showed a visiting American scientist from Stanford University, Siegfried Hecker, an apparently working uranium enrichment plant that the country had been building for years, and that the C.I.A. had missed, though the agency had been right about other secret facilities. The plant gave North Korea a new way to produce nuclear weapons, even as his people fell into another food shortage.

The same year, the North made two attacks against the South Korean military, sinking a ship and later shelling an island near Northern waters. The episodes caused the United States and South Korea to conduct new joint exercises, even while the Chinese, apparently fearing a complete collapse of the North Korean regime, increased its economic aid.

Despite his ill health, he was reported to have visited one of the units that attacked the South, to hand out medals, and recently managed one last visit to his benefactors in China. But it is unclear whether his son and presumed successor accompanied him on the trip.

CHOE SANG-HUN contributed reporting.

CHAPTER 6

A New Leader Brings Renewed Tensions and Diplomacy

Kim Jong-un's assumption of his father's role as Supreme Leader of North Korea left many wondering if the young leader — only 27 years old at the time — would open up the isolated and economically deprived country and improve its human rights record. Thus far, the jury is out. Initially, he further strained diplomatic relations with the United States, South Korea and Japan by increasing his country's nuclear testing. Yet, in 2018, he showed unusual levels of diplomacy, culminating in a June 2018 meeting with U.S. President Donald J. Trump.

At Huge Rally, North Koreans Declare Kim Their Leader

BY CHOE SANG-HUN | DEC. 29, 2011

SEOUL, SOUTH KOREA — The declaration on Thursday that Kim Jong-un is now the "supreme leader" of North Korea was an emotional turning point for the hermetic country — reaffirming support for the young heir after nearly two weeks of national mourning for his father, Kim Jong-il.

The naming of Mr. Kim as supreme leader was partly a formality — all signals have pointed to his taking over both the military and the

ED JONES/AFP/GETTY IMAGES

Kim Jong-un salutes as he watches a military parade in Pyongyang.

powerful Workers' Party — but it was also an important step in the push to strengthen his position in any power struggles that might follow.

Mr. Kim is young — believed to be in his 20s — and untested, making him more vulnerable to challenges.

The announcement on Thursday of Mr. Kim's elevation was made by Kim Yong-nam, the president of the North Korean Parliament, who is considered the ceremonial head of state. It was followed by similar speeches by top party and military officials.

"Respected Comrade Kim Jong-un is now supreme leader of our party, military and people," Kim Yong-nam said, adding that Kim Jong-un "inherits the ideology, leadership, courage and audacity of Comrade Kim Jong-il."

The announcement was made before a crowd of tens of thousands that gathered in a central square in Pyongyang, the North's capital, for the last official day of mourning for Kim Jong-il.

In the past few days, North Korea has showered Kim Jong-un with the honorific titles reserved, until now, for his father: "great leader," "dear leader," "peerless leader," and "the sun of the 21st century." He was even referred to as the nation's parent, a designation that North Korea had used for Kim Jong-il and his father, Kim Il-sung.

The ceremony on Thursday was particularly symbolic of Kim Jong-un's rise to the top leadership post: for the first time since his father's death, he was facing a huge crowd of North Koreans alone — without his father standing by him.

Though North Korea declared Kim Jong-un its top leader throughout the carefully choreographed ceremony, and in the relentless pronouncements of the past week, he has yet to take any official titles, like supreme commander of the 1.2 million-strong Korean People's Army and general secretary of the Workers' Party. Those are bestowed at meetings of top party and government officials, most likely in the coming months, that in the past have been mere formalities.

At noon on Thursday, the country observed three minutes of silence nationwide in memory of Kim Jong-il. Trains and ships sounded their horns, state news media reported. Similar but smaller ceremonies were held in cities across North Korea, the country's official Korean Central News Agency reported.

To Sell a New Leader, North Korea Finds a Mirror Is Handy

BY CHOE SANG-HUN | FEB. 1, 2012

SEOUL, SOUTH KOREA — When Kim Jong-un made his debut as the North Korean heir apparent in September 2010, he looked so much like his grandfather, the closest thing North Koreans had to a god, that South Korean intelligence officials noted that many North Koreans who saw the young man for the first time on television broke down in tears.

"The regime wants its people to see Kim Jong-un as Great Leader Kim Il-sung reincarnated," said Kim Kwang-in, head of the North Korea Strategy Center, a research organization based in Seoul that collects information from sources inside North Korea. "They fattened him up and gave him a thorough training — and plastic surgery, too, some even say — to make him look just like his grandfather."

Since his elevation to leader after the death of his father, Kim Jong-il, in December, Kim Jong-un has been presenting himself as a near replica of his grandfather, Kim Il-sung — from the way he clapped his hands, walked with shoulders thrown back and stood tall with a paunch, down to such details as his double-breasted greatcoat, high-trimmed sideburns, double chin and full cheeks.

The packaging of Mr. Kim as the embodiment of the North's widely revered founding president suggests that a well-oiled machine is at work to create a new leader. The strategy of having Mr. Kim assume his grandfather's persona, and relying on nostalgia for the "Great Leader" to justify and consolidate his dynastic succession, reflects the slightness of the young leader's own résumé, as well as the length of his grandfather's and father's shadows, under which he must rule.

It also suggests a note of desperation among the nomenklatura, who know that their own privileged positions depend on the survival of the Kim dynasty. Whether it will work or not remains an open question.

More immediately, there is fevered speculation here about what kind of leader he will make — a figurehead, another Kim Jong-il or a North Korean Deng Xiaoping.

"When North Koreans see Kim Jong-un, they think of Kim Il-sung when he was 33," said An Chan-il, a former North Korean Army officer.

Mr. An, 57, was referring to 1945, when Kim Il-sung, a guerrilla leader fighting for Korean independence, entered Pyongyang at the end of Japanese colonial rule, casting himself as the smiling liberator. In reality, it was the Americans and the Soviets who liberated Korea from Japan and divided it between them.

"After the hardship of recent years, North Koreans yearn for another liberator," said Mr. An, who defected to the South in 1979 and worked as a government analyst in Seoul before opening his own research group, the World Institute for North Korea Studies, in 2010.

Kim Jong-il was a master propagandist who directed several movies. His last work may have been casting Kim Jong-un as a successor who inherited his father's policy but his grandfather's face. It was a role that Kim Jong-il knew he could never play. He indicated that his homely, pear-shaped looks were loathed by many North Koreans (he once called himself "an ugly midget"), according to South Koreans who met him.

Since Kim Jong-il's death, the North Korean state news media have vowed that Kim Jong-un will faithfully follow his father's songun, or "military first," policy. That approach gives top priority for resource allocations to the military, a linchpin in the father's, and now the son's, efforts to maintain internal unity.

But Kim Jong-il's 17-year rule was marked by floods, drought, mass starvation and deepening international sanctions in response to his nuclear weapons program. In public, he often looked dour and aloof. Groveling generals kept a deferential distance from him. Few ordinary North Koreans ever heard him speak.

By contrast, Kim Jong-un is striking a confident posture that recalls his grandfather, who is often depicted in North Korean textbooks and murals as a leader surrounded by children and workers. Mr. Kim's youthful visage as a new nation-builder came as the regime was promising its long-suffering people "a strong and prosperous nation."

Grinning, sampling soup in a school kitchen, linking arms with workers, clambering onto a tank with soldiers, embracing young pilots rushing to his chest in tears and pulling weathered army generals closer to give them words of advice, Kim Jong-un looks at home in his new role as the national eobeoi, or "parent," as his grandfather and ancient Korean kings were regarded by their subjects.

But things in Pyongyang may not be proceeding as smoothly as they appear.

Kim Jong-un, who is believed to be in his late 20s, has an influential uncle, Jang Song-taek. Mr. Jang serves as Mr. Kim's mentor, but his ambitions beyond that are shrouded in mystery.

Mr. Kim also has a half brother, Kim Jong-nam, who is living in semi-exile in China and is talking regularly to journalists from Japan, North Korea's sworn enemy, to predict doom for his half brother's rule. His daring criticism of Kim Jong-un fueled speculation that China and certain generals in Pyongyang might be protecting him as a hedge should things go wrong with Kim Jong-un's succession. Officially, Beijing has voiced support for Kim Jong-un.

Cheong Seong-chang, an analyst at the Sejong Institute, said he believed that Kim Jong-un had already established himself solidly as successor before his father's death. The generals whom his mother, Ko Young-hee, helped promote before her death in 2004 stood behind him, Mr. Cheong said. But others believe that Mr. Kim remains little more than a figurehead, with the real power belonging to his uncle, Mr. Jang.

If anything, Mr. Kim appears for now to be a figurehead for his dead grandfather and father, many analysts say. In the hybrid Stalinist-Confucian dynasty that his grandfather and father created, he is presented as having a divine right to rule because of his blood ties to Kim Il-sung. That also means that he can risk his own legitimacy as leader if he rejects his father's policies and attempts to introduce radical changes. That same fear haunts the elite, whose vested interests, rooted in their ties to the Kim family, are also conferred by heredity.

That goes a long way toward explaining why the regime has lost no time raising the profile of the young Mr. Kim. Since his father's funeral, he has visited one military unit every four or five days, casting himself as a caring and competent commander and highlighting perhaps his single most important qualification as leader, that he looks more like his grandfather than his unpopular father.

"It looks as if the DNA jumped from grandfather to grandson, skipping the father," said Lee Yun-keol, a North Korean biologist who defected to the South in 2006 and now leads the North Korea Strategic Information Service Center, a private research organization. "So we have a new leader who looks just like his grandpa. But that doesn't change much in the North."

North Korean Leader Stresses Need for Strong Military

BY CHOE SANG-HUN | APRIL 15, 2012

SEOUL, SOUTH KOREA — In his first speech in public since assuming the leadership of North Korea, Kim Jong-un said Sunday that his "first, second and third" priorities were to strengthen the military, and he declared that superiority in military technology was "no longer monopolized by imperialists."

Mr. Kim's speech was followed by what South Korean officials said was the North's biggest display of weapons in a military parade, including a missile the North appeared to be presenting for the first time. While it is not clear whether it was a new long-range missile or a mock-up, its display demonstrates the importance that the North Korean government places on weapons development despite an embarrassing failure of a rocket it launched last week.

South Korean officials would not comment on the North Korean missile, pending further examination.

Mr. Kim's claim to superior military technology could sound poignant, coming two days after the North Korean rocket carrying a satellite disintegrated in midair. The failure of the rocket indicated that North Korea might still have a long way to go before mastering the technology to deliver warheads atop an intercontinental ballistic missile.

Mr. Kim's speech on the 100th birthday of Kim Il-sung, his grandfather and the North's founding president, was his public political debut. In an unexpected 20-minute speech, broadcast live inside North Korea, Mr. Kim demonstrated a new leadership style but reaffirmed his adherence to the "military first" policy of his father, Kim Jong-il, which has left North Korea locked in a prolonged confrontation with the United States and its allies.

His speech was a major departure from the practices of his reclusive father, who cloaked his brutal rule in mystery and who never gave a speech to the general public before his death in December. North Koreans did not even hear Kim Jong-il's voice until a broadcast in 1992, when he shouted one sentence into the microphone while inspecting a military parade: "Glory to the heroic soldiers of the People's Army."

On Sunday, facing tens of thousands gathered in a plaza in the capital, Pyongyang, Mr. Kim did not mention the rocket failure. Instead, he exhorted his people to appreciate the achievements of his father and grandfather, crediting them with developing nuclear weapons as a deterrent against American invasion.

"The days are gone forever when our enemies could blackmail us with nuclear bombs," he said.

Mr. Kim has been seen but not heard by the public since taking over after his father's death. A thunderous cheer erupted when he appeared on the podium, waving a hand at the crowd gathered beneath in neat rows for the meticulously choreographed festivities. Thousands of balloons were released.

ED JONES/AFP/GETTY IMAGES

North Korean soldiers march during a military parade in Pyongyang on April 15, 2012, to mark the 100th birthday of the late Kim Il-sung.

An emotional North Korean television broadcaster marveled at how the young leader had "the look and voice" of his charismatic grandfather, who is much revered in the North. Reading a prepared text, Mr. Kim spoke in a calm, measured and somewhat husky voice, occasionally looking up from the text to squint at the crowd under the sun.

The only gesture he made was when he raised a finger to emphasize the last sentence of his speech: "Let's go on for our final victory."

Analysts said that Mr. Kim's physical resemblance to his grandfather, his gregariousness in the public eye — easily mixing with soldiers, workers and aging generals — and even his willingness to address the nation on state television were carefully cultivated assets for a leader in his late 20s hoping to give his government a more youthful appeal. (The portraits of Marx and Lenin that once adorned prominent buildings in Pyongyang were taken down ahead of the Sunday celebrations, The Associated Press reported from the North Korean capital.)

Cheong Seong-chang of the Sejong Institute, a private research institute in South Korea, said Mr. Kim's performance reminded North Koreans of Kim Il-sung, who as a young leader used to meet citizens and give public speeches. "Kim Jong-il inspired awe and dread among his people and was never a leader friendly with the public," Mr. Cheong said. "Like his grandfather, however, Kim Jong-un has so far tried to look more willing to communicate with his people. We may see him speak in public more often."

Sunday's speech and parade were the culmination of weeks of festivities intended to infuse the North Koreans with pride that their country, as its propagandists put it, has become a military power despite decades of economic hardship.

"Yesterday, we were a weak and small country trampled upon by big powers," Mr. Kim said. "Today, our geopolitical location remains the same, but we are transformed into a proud political and military power and an independent people that no one can dare provoke."

He said he was determined to make sure that his people "will never have to tighten their belt again." Yet he did not offer concrete economic programs, other than a vague reference to the need for an "industrial revolution." Neither did he mention that his rocket launching had led to the cancellation of badly needed American food aid.

The United States and its allies have called for censuring North Korea at the United Nations Security Council. But China appealed for all sides to "remain calm and exercise restraint" on Sunday after its foreign minister, Yang Jiechi, talked with Secretary of State Hillary Rodham Clinton and the South Korean foreign minister, Kim Sung-hwan, in separate telephone conversations.

Some analysts say that the insecurity created by the rocket failure may push Kim Jong-un to rely more heavily on the military and attempt an even more provocative nuclear test in an effort to be taken seriously. The Korean People's Army, with about 1.1 million troops, has become the backbone of political power under Kim Jong-il's "military first" policy.

Kim Jong-un "is not secure enough" to endorse a possible demand from moderates in his government for policy shifts after the rocket debacle, said Chang Yong-seok, a senior researcher at Seoul National University's Institute for Peace and Unification Studies. "He still relies on his dead father's authority to justify his rule."

Hours after the failure of the rocket marred his ascension to North Korea's highest posts, Mr. Kim promoted 70 officers to the rank of general, the North's main ruling party newspaper, Rodong Sinmun, reported Saturday.

Mr. Kim ordered the promotions as one of his first actions after becoming chairman of the National Defense Commission. The post was the last of the top military, party and state titles he has inherited from his father.

North Korea's Leader Is Said to Oust Uncle in Power Play

BY CHOE SANG-HUN AND DAVID E. SANGER | DEC. 3, 2013

SEOUL, SOUTH KOREA — Kim Jong-un, the 30-year-old leader of North Korea, came to power two years ago so inexperienced and untested that the reclusive government named his uncle as the North Korean equivalent of a regent to watch over him.

On Tuesday, the National Intelligence Service of South Korea reported that the uncle, Jang Song-thaek, had been stripped of his powers, apparently by the young leader he was supposed to supervise. It was the biggest in a series of purges, promotions and reshufflings of elites that seem to have remade the government in the image of Mr. Kim, who inherited his title, and apparently techniques for keeping the government in control, from his father and grandfather.

The political changes, which were not announced by North Korea and could not be independently confirmed, follow a series of upheavals, especially within the military. American intelligence officials and some outside analysts speculate that Mr. Kim is sidelining the stalwarts of his father, Kim Jong-il, and elevating a new set of generals and party officials who owe their loyalty only to him. But there are also hints, one American intelligence official said, that "there was some kind of broader contest for control, which Jang lost, at least for now."

Early in the young Mr. Kim's tenure, American intelligence assessments questioned whether he would have the staying power to remain in office, and said he was regarded by the North Korean military as spoiled and naïve.

Two years later those assessments are reversing. He is now seen as fully in charge. Mr. Kim has already begun testing the loyalty of top officials by dismissing or demoting them and letting them try to win his favor again — often by spying against others, another technique of leadership inherited from his father, according to South Korean officials and analysts.

Mr. Jang's apparent fall from power came after his two deputies at the administrative department of the ruling Workers' Party of Korea were executed last month on charges of "corruption and anti-party activities," according to South Korean lawmakers who were briefed by intelligence officials in a hurriedly scheduled meeting at the National Assembly in Seoul.

The intelligence agency did not reveal how it learned of the executions, the lawmakers said.

"I don't think Jang's deputies were executed for mere corruption. Rather, they were executed because they established a 'power,' " said Cheong Seong-chang, a senior analyst at Sejong Institute in South Korea.

Despite initial hints that Mr. Kim might seek a more cooperative relationship with the country's neighbors and the United States, he has accompanied political changes at home with a hard-line nationalistic policy of accelerating the country's nuclear program, the main card it has to play in international negotiations.

In February, North Korea conducted its third nuclear test, and it appears to be restarting its capacity to produce plutonium, a main ingredient for its small nuclear arsenal. And it has threatened to attack Japanese, South Korean and American targets, though in recent months the country's warnings of imminent war have quieted.

The reported downfall of Mr. Jang, effectively North Korea's No. 2 leader, set off a frenzy of speculation among North Korea watchers and South Korean government officials. Since Mr. Kim took power, they have theorized that a power and policy struggle might be playing out behind the public displays of mass solidarity. Mr. Jang's rise in power in the past few years coincided with the humiliation of the old military elite, who surrendered some of their lucrative rights to trade in minerals and seafood to the cabinet and the party, where Mr. Jang has built his career.

Some analysts said they feared that the eclipse of Mr. Jang so early in Mr. Kim's rule could suggest a power struggle that could destabilize the North. If so, they worry that Mr. Kim might resort to militaristic provocations to divert attention from domestic instability.

On Tuesday, the Defense Ministry in Seoul said it saw no unusual movement from the North Korean Army.

"Jang Song-thaek and his wife, Kim Kyong-hee, have been the core members of power upholding Kim Jong-un, and I think Jang's fall will entail a serious shake-up in the North Korean political landscape," Jeong Cheong-rae, a South Korean opposition lawmaker and member of the National Assembly's intelligence committee, said Tuesday. "The intelligence agency gave us an unexpected briefing today, saying that they had something urgent to report about a development of great import in North Korea."

In the past, North Korean officials reported to have been purged in South Korean media have resurfaced. Mr. Jang himself had disappeared twice in the past but later staged a comeback. Still, even before the South Korea intelligence report, his unusually long absence from North Korean media was viewed by the news media in the South as a sign that he was in trouble.

"The latest purge or execution of Jang's followers sends a powerful message to all and particularly to those harboring illusions of power," said Sung-yoon Lee, North Korea specialist at the Fletcher School of Law and Diplomacy at Tufts University.

"In a totalitarian system, the life of the No. 2 man or regent is oftentimes short and precarious," Mr. Lee added.

Mr. Jang, 67, has been a fixture in the North Korean power elite since the days of Kim Jong-il, exercising his widespread influence from the party's administrative department, which he headed. His wife is the sister of Kim Jong-il and an aunt of the current leader.

The couple emerged as key brokers of power after Kim Jong-il suffered a stroke in 2008. They played leading roles in engineering the fast-track grooming of Kim Jong-un as designated heir, analysts said.

After Kim Jong-il's death in late 2011, the couple helped their nephew consolidate power through a series of purges that replaced 44 percent of top officials in the party, military and cabinet. (Mr. Jang is estranged from his ailing wife, according to reports in the South Korean news media.)

Outside news outlets have since called Mr. Jang a "guardian" and "mentor" for his young nephew. In April, Pak Pong-ju, an economic technocrat reportedly close to Mr. Jang, was made premier, a post that includes oversight of the economy. Last year, Mr. Jang visited China to seek Beijing's help in building two free economic zones on its border.

But Mr. Jang's seemingly unbridled influence has also prompted analysts to speculate that Mr. Kim would eventually see him as a challenge to his authority. They said that Mr. Kim had moved to weaken the broad network Mr. Jang had built while the regime was going through a transition in the last two years.

Mr. Jang would not be the first No. 2 or the first uncle of the North Korean leader to lose power. Kim Jong-il plotted a purge of his own powerful uncle to solidify control after the death of his father, the North's founding president, Kim Il-sung.

In July last year, Kim Jong-un removed his then No. 2 man, Vice Marshal Ri Yong-ho.

Analysts said they suspected that Mr. Jang's downfall may have been engineered by Kim Won-hong, who was made head of the nation's secret police and spy agency in April last year, and Vice Marshal Choe Ryong-hae, who became the top political officer in the military under Mr. Kim. On Tuesday, the South Korean intelligence officials said North Korea's secret police began investigating the corruption of Mr. Jang's close allies this year.

When Mr. Jang vanished from public view before, the last time from 2003 to 2006, it was during a period when Mr. Kim's father suppressed his power. He was humbled and later reinstated, according to South Korean officials.

U.S. Confronts Consequences of Underestimating North Korean Leader

BY DAVID E. SANGER | APRIL 24, 2014

SEOUL, SOUTH KOREA — Almost everything American intelligence agencies and North Korea-watchers thought they understood two years ago about Kim Jong-un, the North's young leader, turns out to have been wrong.

The briefings given to President Obama after Mr. Kim inherited leadership said it was almost certain he would be kept in check by his more experienced uncle, Jang Song-thaek. Instead, Mr. Kim had his uncle and dozens of others executed.

The early betting was also that Mr. Kim, who was briefly educated in Switzerland, would emphasize economic overhaul over expanding the nuclear and missile arsenals that were his father's and grandfather's legacy. Instead, the nuclear program has surged forward, and recent missile tests are demonstrating that after years of spectacular failures, the North's engineers are finally improving their aim. Their next big challenge is proving that an intercontinental missile they have shown only in mock-ups can reach America's shores.

As a result, when Mr. Obama lands here on Friday on the second stop of his Asia tour, he will be confronting the question of whether his strategy of "strategic patience" with the North has been overtaken by reality: an unpredictable, though calculating, ruler in Mr. Kim, who has proved to be more ruthless, aggressive and tactically skilled than anyone expected.

"We have failed," said Evans J. R. Revere, who spent his State Department career trying various diplomatic strategies to stop the North. "For two decades our policy has been to keep the North Koreans from developing nuclear weapons. It's now clear there is no way they will give them up, no matter what sanctions we impose, no matter what we offer. So now what?"

It is an assessment some of Mr. Obama's aides say they privately share, though for now the administration refuses to negotiate with the North until it first fulfills its oft-violated agreements to freeze its nuclear and missile programs. A recent effort inside the National Security Council to devise a new approach resulted in a flurry of papers and classified strategy sessions — and the conclusion that all the alternatives to the current course were worse.

"We're stuck," one participant in the review said.

The only place any real change is visible is in the military planning by South Korea and the United States, which maintains a shrunken force of 28,000 troops in the South. For the first time since the armistice in 1953, officials say, the contingency plan for a conflict with the North treats the nation as a nuclear-capable adversary, despite the administration's official refusal to acknowledge it as a de facto nuclear state. (What appear to be North Korea's preparations for a fourth nuclear test, perhaps in the coming days, seem intended to remove all doubt.)

The latest revision of OpPlan 5029, the war plan for the Korean Peninsula, assumes that if a conflict broke out, the North would be able to deliver a crude nuclear weapon, though perhaps by truck or ship. American intelligence officials do not believe the North is yet able to shrink a bomb to a size that could fit on one of its Nodong missiles, the key breakthrough it needs.

"He's put new effort into his nuclear program, missiles, special operations forces and long-range artillery," said Gen. Curtis M. Scaparrotti, who took over last fall as commander of United States Forces Korea and the United Nations Command here. "They are using more underground facilities. He's gone to school on how we operate."

Defense officials say they now have less warning time on missile launchings than they had two or three years ago because Mr. Kim has put his resources into mobile launchers that are regularly moved from tunnel to tunnel, making them harder for American satellites to track.

Although details of the revised plan are classified, officials have talked about elements of it. Since the North shelled a South Korean island and was blamed for sinking a South Korean warship four years ago, there are now extensive plans for immediately responding to and then de-escalating small attacks along the border regions.

The North Korean forces remain numerically impressive at a million soldiers, but highly unimpressive when they train. The country is so poor that South Korean military officials say its pilots rarely have the gas to perform practice runs.

But in recent interviews here and in Washington, a picture has emerged of Mr. Kim's new focus on inexpensive weaponry, from missile launchers to crude cyberweapons, that are hard to detect and harder to halt. Mr. Kim, who is believed to be 30 years old, has also nurtured his reputation for unpredictability, keeping adversaries on edge.

Administration officials acknowledge they have largely left North Korea on the back burner while focusing on sanctions, cyberattacks and pressure on Iran, forcing it into negotiations.

"The administration decided, consciously or implicitly, that Iran was more important and there was a greater prospect of getting something done," said Robert Einhorn, who ran the sanctions enforcement program against both countries until he left the State Department last year. "While you can squeeze Iran and its oil money, it's much harder to squeeze North Korea" while China continues its financial support.

White House officials argue that focusing first on Iran made sense. Its program can still be halted before it gains a weapons ability, if that is Tehran's goal, and the administration believes that North Korea is less likely to set off a regional arms race.

"You could argue that the best North Korea strategy now is to get a deal with Iran, and use it as a model for the North about what the world can look like," one senior administration official said.

But others inside the administration fear that policy is too passive — and perhaps a prescription for a much larger North Korean arsenal by the time Mr. Obama leaves office.

At the heart of the problem are dashed hopes that Mr. Kim would conclude that his grandfather's and father's pursuit of a nuclear ability was a

Cold War relic, and that he would gradually steer the country to integration with the world economy. There was modest reason for optimism just months after Mr. Kim came to power in 2011 and struck yet another deal to freeze all his nuclear and missile activity, in return for a resumption of the episodic six-party talks with the United States and other nations. That brief effort ended when the North launched a satellite in honor of Mr. Kim's grandfather. Diplomacy froze for the next two years, with the administration unwilling to make concessions as previous administrations did only to find that the North was reneging on its promises.

In recent months the Chinese have led an effort to restart diplomatic talks, and the United States has quietly met with the North. But the goal is unclear. To the United States, the purpose of the talks would be denuclearization; Mr. Kim's government has already declared that the one thing he will not do is give up his small nuclear arsenal, especially after seeing the United States help unseat Col. Muammar el-Qaddafi of Libya, who surrendered his own nuclear program in 2003.

Joel Wit, a former North Korea strategist for the American government, said Mr. Kim drew an indelible lesson from that history. "It's not an accident he's positioning himself to make sure the inventory of nuclear material in the hands of the North is about to take off," said Mr. Wit, who edits 38 North, a website that follows the murky, often murderous politics of the Kim government.

He was referring to the North's effort to expand the production of highly enriched uranium, which would give Mr. Kim a steadier, more plentiful supply of nuclear fuel than its past reliance on extracting plutonium from a small nuclear reactor.

"I'm now convinced North Korea would prefer to collapse with nuclear weapons than try to survive without nuclear weapons," Chun Yung-woo, who recently served as the South's national security adviser, said this week. Yet the strategy Washington is pursuing is based on the opposite assumption.

Kim Jong-un's Claim of North Korea Hydrogen Bomb Draws Skepticism

BY CHOE SANG-HUN | DEC. 10, 2015

SEOUL, SOUTH KOREA — The North Korean leader, Kim Jong-un, said his country had developed a hydrogen bomb, its state-run media said Thursday. The claim was the latest of several that the isolated country has made about its nuclear capabilities that outside analysts have greeted with skepticism.

The North's official Korean Central News Agency said Mr. Kim had made the assertion during a visit to the Phyongchon Revolutionary Site, which honors the works of his father and grandfather, who ruled North Korea before him.

KCNA/XINHUA/ALAMY LIVE NEWS

Kim Jong-un at the Phyongchon Revolutionary Site on December 10, 2015, the day he announced that his country developed a hydrogen bomb.

His forebears' work turned North Korea into "a powerful nuclear weapons state ready to detonate a self-reliant A-bomb and H-bomb to reliably defend its sovereignty and the dignity of the nation," Mr. Kim was quoted as saying.

The White House on Thursday said it was doubtful that North Korea had developed a hydrogen bomb.

"At this point, the information that we have access to calls into serious question those claims, but we take very seriously the risk and the threat that is posed by the North Korean regime in their ambitions to develop a nuclear weapon," Josh Earnest, the White House press secretary, told reporters, according to Reuters.

Although the report was the first time Mr. Kim had claimed that the North had developed a hydrogen bomb, several years ago a state-run newspaper asserted that the North may have been trying to build one. In May 2010, the front page of Rodong Sinmun, North Korea's top state-run newspaper, declared that its scientists had succeeded in creating a nuclear fusion reaction, a crucial technology for creating a hydrogen bomb.

At the time, many observers ridiculed the claim by North Korea, which often uses bombastic assertions to increase leverage over its enemies in negotiations or to burnish its image at home. But the claim was never completely dismissed.

Hwang Jang-yop, a former secretary of North Korea's ruling Workers' Party who defected to Seoul in 1997, said the North had long researched nuclear fusion while trying to build a hydrogen bomb, as well as atomic weapons. Mr. Hwang died in October 2010.

North Korea conducted underground tests to set off nuclear devices in 2006, 2009 and 2013. It has since claimed to have developed "diversified" and "miniaturized" nuclear devices, but Western experts remain unsure.

On Thursday, South Korean officials said that there was no evidence that the North had hydrogen bomb capacity. But they also noted that North Korea has repeatedly vowed to improve its nuclear arsenal, which is believed to include several weapons, though none as destructive as a hydrogen bomb.

In a paper published in May, Lee Chun-keun, a senior researcher at the Science and Technology Policy Institute of South Korea, said North Korea acquired laser nuclear fusion equipment from China in the 1980s and that it might be developing a reinforced nuclear weapon from nuclear fusion.

"Tests of such an advanced atomic weapon can be done in a lab without an actual nuclear explosion," he wrote. "Further development of nuclear fusion technology would lead to the development of reinforced atomic arms and furthermore hydrogen bomb developments as well."

Making a true hydrogen bomb is very difficult. But weapon designers can easily boost the destructive power of an atom bomb by putting at its core a small amount of tritium, a radioactive form of hydrogen.

In a paper published by the Institute for Science and International Security in Washington in September, David Albright and Serena Kelleher-Vergantini said that North Korea might be trying to use the only operational reactor at its main nuclear complex in Yongbyon, north of Pyongyang, to produce tritium.

"Tritium would enable nuclear weapons designs that could have a greater explosive yield than weapons made from only plutonium or weapon-grade uranium," they wrote. "Whether North Korea can make nuclear weapons using tritium is unknown although we believe that it remains a technical problem North Korea still needs to solve."

Kim Jong-un's Image Shift: From Nuclear Madman to Skillful Leader

BY CHOE SANG-HUN | JUNE 6, 2018

SEOUL, SOUTH KOREA — He ordered his uncle executed and half brother assassinated. He spent millions developing and testing a hydrogen bomb and intercontinental ballistic missiles as his people suffered severe food shortages. He exchanged threats of nuclear annihilation with President Trump, calling the American leader a "mentally deranged U.S. dotard."

That was last year's image.

In more recent months, North Korea's leader, Kim Jong-un, has achieved one of the most striking transformations in modern diplomacy.

The man described by critics as a murderous dictator and nuclear lunatic has held hands and had heart-to-heart talks with South Korea's president, Moon Jae-in, who has encouraged and abetted Mr. Kim's makeover.

Mr. Kim has enticed South Korea and the United States into negotiations by dangling the possibility of denuclearizing his country. His popularity has surged in polls in South Korea as he prepares to become the first North Korean leader to meet a sitting American president.

With a dazzle of diplomatic initiatives in the run-up to his historic June 12 summit meeting with Mr. Trump in Singapore, Mr. Kim has effectively redefined himself. Some South Koreans now see him as more reliable than Mr. Trump despite the decades-long alliance between their country and the United States.

Mr. Kim's enhanced standing among South Koreans was crystallized by recent images of him walking in the woods with Mr. Moon, and on a beach with President Xi Jinping of China discussing North Korea's nuclear program.

The optics contrasted with what many South Koreans view as Mr. Trump's scattershot diplomacy, in which he abruptly canceled the Singapore summit meeting, then reversed himself after Mr. Kim authorized a calm statement offering Mr. Trump "time and opportunity" to change his mind. (On Wednesday, one of the president's lawyers, Rudolph W. Giuliani, said that Mr. Kim "got back on his hands and knees and begged" for the meeting to be rescheduled.)

Despite the image change, Mr. Kim is unlikely to surrender his nuclear weapons anytime soon, or ease the grip of his repressive regime. But he has proved to be a skilled — some might say beguiling — strategist, driving events on the Korean Peninsula and showing a willingness to recalibrate.

"Once Kim Jong-un decided to improve ties with South Korea and the United States, he knew he could not do so with his image as a repressive tyrant," said Kang Dong-wan, an expert on North Korea's "image politics" at Dong-A University in Busan, South Korea. "He is creating a new portrait of him abroad as the leader of a normal country."

In the West, Mr. Kim, 34, has often been caricatured as a chubby child toying with nuclear missiles. Mr. Trump, more than twice his age, has called Mr. Kim "short and fat," a "sick puppy" and a "little rocket man."

But when Mr. Trump meets Mr. Kim, the American leader will be dealing with the ruler of a totalitarian regime adept at political theatrics to bolster Mr. Kim's charisma at home and advance his agenda abroad.

"The reason the world pays attention to him is not just because he has a few nuclear weapons, but more because of his image as a leader with mystical power, his absolute control over a highly consolidated, regimented and disciplined country," said Chung Byung-ho, an anthropologist at Hanyang University in South Korea, who examined the role of theatrics in North Korean politics in a book he wrote with another scholar.

Whatever his true personality, Mr. Kim has found an avid partner in advancing his new image: Mr. Moon.

Since taking office a year ago, Mr. Moon has exhorted Mr. Trump to test the idea that Mr. Kim was a reasonable leader ready to bargain away his nuclear weapons for the right incentives, such as normalized ties and security assurances from the United States. It seems to have worked: Mr. Trump has recently changed his public appraisals of the North Korean leader, calling him "smart and gracious" and "very honorable."

Mr. Kim started his image makeover this year by reaching out to South Korea, which was eager to play intermediary between North Korea and the United States after a year in which the countries appeared to verge on war. In a New Year's Day speech, Mr. Kim offered to send athletes, cheerleaders and political emissaries to South Korea during its Winter Olympics.

Then, he whetted Washington's appetite for negotiations by announcing a moratorium on nuclear and missile tests, closing North Korea's only known nuclear test site and releasing three American prisoners. He also appeared to have hedged his bets by meeting twice with Mr. Xi, mending frayed ties with an old ally whose protection he needed as he entered delicate negotiations with Washington. The diplomatic outreach was a sharp departure from North Korea's history of rhetorical bombast, chest-thumping theatrics, military parades and mass rallies, which have fed the country's image as an international pariah.

Mr. Kim's image reinvention was skillfully staged with the help of Mr. Moon's government, which made sure every detail of the leaders' April 27 summit meeting was steeped in potent symbols dear to both Koreas: respect, ethnic unity and eventual Korean reunification.

For the meeting held at the "truce village" of Panmunjom on the inter-Korean border, Mr. Moon's government redecorated a conference building, installing paintings of famous mountains and waterfalls that reminded people in both Koreas of their shared heritage before their peninsula was divided by foreign powers at the end of World War II.

"We packed each piece of furniture and each painting with a story," said Koh Min-jeong, a spokeswoman for Mr. Moon.

During a break from their talks, Mr. Kim and Mr. Moon ambled off for a walk through the woods of Panmunjom, with cameras broadcasting their outing live around the world.

But nothing softened Mr. Kim's image like the moment when he arrived at the border to meet with Mr. Moon. At Mr. Kim's suggestion, Mr. Moon stepped across the border into the North for 10 seconds. Then Mr. Kim and Mr. Moon walked back across to the South for their meeting, holding hands, an encounter that transfixed television viewers in South Korea.

"That single gesture went beyond political language," said Mr. Chung, the anthropologist. "The theatrics conveyed messages of trust that language alone could not."

The summit meeting mainly rehashed old inter-Korean agreements that had never been kept, producing only a vaguely worded commitment to denuclearization and peace. But the images made the event a success, providing momentum for warmed ties between the two countries and redefining Mr. Kim in the eyes of many South Koreans.

The next morning, a South Korean newspaper filled its front and back pages with a photograph showing Mr. Moon and Mr. Kim crossing the border hand in hand. Mr. Kim, formerly vilified as the region's most dangerous leader, was considered "trustworthy" by 77 percent of South Koreans following the meeting, according to a survey by the Korea Research Center.

"Chairman Kim's popularity has risen rapidly among South Koreans, and so have the expectations," Mr. Moon told Mr. Kim last month when they met for the second time at Panmunjom. He said the summit meeting especially strengthened Mr. Kim's image among younger South Koreans, who have shaped their views of North Korea through the past decade of inter-Korean tensions and have become increasingly skeptical of reconciliation, much less reunification, with the North.

"That's great to hear," Mr. Kim responded, according to South Korean officials.

Critics warn of dashed expectations, reiterating their view that Mr. Kim will never completely abandon the nuclear weapons considered so dear to his regime's survival and his legitimacy as leader of North Korea.

"It's right to be skeptical," said Ra Jong-yil, a political scientist and former deputy director of the South's National Intelligence Service. "How can the leader of a nation change so quickly? We tend to see what we want to see in North Korea."

Some expect that in his meeting with Mr. Trump, Mr. Kim will most likely commit to denuclearizing his country completely in order to weaken the rationale for sanctions, but insist on a "phased" denuclearization. They say Mr. Kim probably fears that whatever agreement he strikes with Mr. Trump may not survive, given Washington's unpredictable politics.

"The whole world is being duped" by Mr. Kim, said Shim Jin-sup, a retired psychological warfare officer of the South Korean military and expert on North Korean propaganda.

Trump and Kim Arrive in Singapore for Historic Summit Meeting

BY MOTOKO RICH | JUNE 10, 2018

SINGAPORE — Fresh from a contentious global economic summit meeting with United States' oldest and closest allies, President Trump arrived in Singapore on Sunday for his historic on-again-off-again meeting with the North Korea leader, Kim Jong-un.

With the nuclear future of North Korea and the security of the entire region at stake, the encounter will be the first ever between a sitting American president and a North Korean leader.

Just over two weeks ago, it seemed that the summit meeting was not going to happen. A few months ago, the two countries even seemed close to the brink of war.

But on Sunday, Mr. Trump arrived just after 8:20 p.m. local time at Paya Lebar Air Base in Singapore aboard Air Force One, a few hours after Mr. Kim landed at Changi Airport on a commercial Air China plane.

Mr. Trump, who has declared that he did not need to prepare for the two-day meeting, will pit his negotiating skills against the leader of one of the world's most isolated countries. Some analysts fear it will be a meeting of mismatched expectations, with Mr. Trump expecting denuclearization from North Korea in return for helping the impoverished nation improve its economy.

Mr. Trump has questioned the need for a strong American military presence in Northeast Asia. Most analysts do not believe that Mr. Kim is prepared to give up his weapons.

But as part of his trust-building steps to get the United States to the table, Mr. Kim appeared to blow up his country's nuclear test site, in Punggye-ri in northeastern North Korea, in May, and said he would put a moratorium on long-range missile tests.

Mr. Trump flew straight from the Group of 7 meeting in Canada, where he had cut short his attendance and then refused to join a joint statement with the allies, threatening to ratchet up his trade war and calling the prime minister of Canada, one of America's closest neighbors and allies, "very dishonest and weak."

This is the farthest Mr. Kim has traveled since taking power in 2011. He arrives after making a striking transformation from what many saw as a despotic, impulsive young leader with a nuclear arsenal to a skilled diplomat who lured South Korea and the United States into negotiations by dangling the possibility of denuclearization.

The North Korean leader and Mr. Trump are scheduled to meet at 9 a.m. on Tuesday, after a dramatic two-week run-up during which Mr. Trump declared that the summit meeting was off and then on again. It was resuscitated at the last minute.

Earlier Sunday, reporters scrambled to track three planes headed from Pyongyang, the North Korean capital, to Singapore. Mr. Kim landed a little after 2:30 p.m. and was greeted at the airport by Singapore's foreign minister, Vivian Balakrishnan.

Mr. Balakrishnan confirmed the arrival in a Twitter post that included a photo of his welcoming Mr. Kim. The foreign minister also greeted Mr. Trump when the president arrived at the air base.

The international news media have descended on Singapore, with the United States, Japan and South Korea sending the most journalists. According to Singapore's Ministry of Communications, about 2,500 journalists have registered to cover the meeting.

A contingent of reporters spent the steaming hot day staking out the St. Regis Hotel, where Mr. Kim's motorcade arrived shortly after 3:30 p.m. with North Korean flags flapping on the front hoods of Mercedes-Benz stretch cars. Traffic was snarled along roads leading to and from the hotel.

The summit meeting will be held at the Capella Resort on Sentosa Island, a popular recreation spot off the southern tip of Singapore.

Although there were nowhere near royal-wedding-level crowds, curious onlookers joined camera crews and journalists on the road outside the St. Regis to watch Mr. Kim's motorcade depart for a meeting with the prime minister of Singapore, Lee Hsien Loong.

"It is a big thing for Singapore," said Patrick Han, 29, an energy research analyst who came out with his mother to wait near the St. Regis on Sunday afternoon. But after seeing how Mr. Trump had alienated allies at the G-7 meeting, Mr. Han said, "I am not really hopeful that a single summit will have tangible results."

Ruairi Gogan, an American who has lived in Singapore for 20 years, began tracking Mr. Kim's flight on flightradar24.com on Saturday.

"He is like Dr. Evil," Mr. Gogan quipped while waiting near the St. Regis, though he added that the summit meeting "might be a good thing."

The St. Regis is less than half a mile from the Shangri La Hotel, where Mr. Trump is staying. But while the Shangri La is set on a residential stretch of road, the St. Regis sits on a busy commercial boulevard next to a run-down strip mall with two money changers, a pet store and "Maids R Us," a hiring agency.

There were road cordons and a heavy police presence outside the St. Regis, although officers took a gentle approach when urging those who had gathered outside the hotel with smartphones and video cameras to move back from the wire barricades.

Outside the Shangri La, about two hours before Mr. Trump was scheduled to land, the road was deserted except for a few bystanders.

Stanley Peck, 49, a doctor who lives nearby and was finishing up an evening run, stopped to snap a photo of a large sign with a silhouette of a machine-gun-toting police officer just outside the entrance to the hotel. "Police checks comply with orders," the sign read.

"It is interesting to know that a small country like ours can have these two big boxers coming in for a fight," Mr. Peck said. "We are proud to host something like this."

Given that just two weeks ago the summit meeting had been canceled, Mr. Peck said, the prospects for the meeting had already "come a long way." He added, "At least they are here and at least they get to shake hands. Hopefully."

Across the city, Singapore has tightened security for the long-awaited meeting. According to Kasiviswanathan Shanmugam, Singapore's minister for home affairs, about 5,000 police officers and emergency responders are on duty throughout the events.

Already, he said, one traveler from a "regional country" was turned away at the airport on Saturday. Immigration and customs officers had stopped the man after determining that he was "behaving very nervously," Mr. Shanmugam said.

"He couldn't answer their questions," Mr. Shanmugam said at a news briefing on Sunday. "They checked his mobile phone and saw that he's been checking through and visiting sites on suicide bombings, and they made an assessment" that he should be barred from entering Singapore.

Mr. Shanmugam said "two or three" other individuals had also been barred from entering the country in recent days.

At the international media center, at Singapore's Formula One Racing Center, journalists gathered in a building overlooking a racetrack to wait for the arrival of Mr. Kim and Mr. Trump.

Some locals were capitalizing on the attention. In a dining hall set up for reporters, the Common Good Company, a consortium of Singaporean food businesses, gave away ice cream in flavors like Kimchi (in honor of Korea) and Durian, a Southeast Asian fruit.

Playing on the themes of the summit meeting, the company displayed signs saying, "Durians May Be Thorny but Relations Needn't Be" and "Feeling More Trump-ish or Kim-ish today?"

James Kwan, a co-director of Common Good, said the company had decided just five days ago to offer the summit-themed items. "We are doing what we can to facilitate peace through food," he said.

Atrocities Under Kim Jong-un: Indoctrination, Prison Gulags, Executions

BY MAYA SALAM AND MATTHEW HAAG | JUNE 11, 2018

WITH THE MEETING of President Trump and Kim Jong-un of North Korea on Tuesday in Singapore, human rights groups are watching for Mr. Trump to bring up North Korea's widespread crimes against humanity.

Mr. Kim rules with extreme brutality, making his nation among the worst human rights violators in the world.

In North Korea, these crimes "entail extermination, murder, enslavement, torture, imprisonment, rape, forced abortions and other sexual violence, persecution on political, religious, racial and gender grounds, the forcible transfer of populations, the enforced disappearance of persons and the inhumane act of knowingly causing prolonged starvation," concluded a 2014 United Nations report that examined North Korea.

Here are some of the atrocities that have happened there.

A NETWORK OF PRISON GULAGS

Many North Koreans live in fear. That is by design, and it is reinforced by the country's ruthless police state.

People accused of political crimes are arrested and sentenced to prison camps without trials, while their families are often kept in the dark about their whereabouts. Up to 120,000 inmates were in the country's four major political prisons in 2014 and were subjected to gruesome conditions, according to the United Nations report.

Prisoners are starved, forced to work, tortured and raped. Reproductive rights are denied through forced abortions and infanticide. Some are executed — sometimes in public. Hundreds of thousands of political prisoners have died in the camps over the past 50 years, the United Nations report found.

In addition to the political camps, North Korea also operates prisons for those accused of ordinary crimes. Some prisons are short-term labor camps. Others hold prisoners who face long-term torture, starvation and other suffering.

MR. KIM'S ENEMIES, AND FAMILY, HAVE BEEN EXECUTED

Since Mr. Kim assumed power in 2011, taking over from his father, Kim Jong-il, he has consolidated his power through executions. In the first six years as leader, he has ordered the executions of at least 340 people, according to the Institute for National Security Strategy, a think tank arm of the National Intelligence Service.

In 2016, Kim Yong-jin, the deputy premier for education, was killed in front of a firing squad after showing "disrespectful posture" in a meeting. Hyon Yong-chol, a general over the armed forces, fell asleep in a meeting. He was executed with an antiaircraft gun.

Family is also not off limits. One of Mr. Kim's uncles, Jang Song-thaek, was convicted of treason. He was then executed with antiaircraft machine guns, and his body incinerated with flamethrowers.

Kim Jong-nam, the estranged brother of the North Korean leader, was killed last year in a very public way: near a check-in counter at Kuala Lumpur International Airport in Malaysia. Two women were seen on security cameras walking up to him and rubbing a substance on his face — a chemical warfare agent known as VX, the United States later determined.

Kim Jong-nam was dead within minutes. The women were arrested, but the United States said evidence showed that North Korea was responsible for the attack.

'AN ALL-ENCOMPASSING INDOCTRINATION MACHINE'

Often the first human rights violations Westerners ascribe to North Korea, aside from preventing North Koreans from leaving the country, are the lengths it takes to indoctrinate its citizens.

According to the United Nations report, which was prepared by its

Commission of Inquiry and is more than 300 pages long, North Korea "operates an all-encompassing indoctrination machine that takes root from childhood to propagate an official personality cult and to manufacture absolute obedience" to Mr. Kim.

Independent thought is bred out and propaganda glorifying the state is plentiful, the report said, as is propaganda intended to "incite nationalistic hatred toward official enemies" like Japan and the United States.

CHRISTIANITY IS DEEMED A 'SERIOUS THREAT'

North Korea considers the spread of most religions dangerous, but Christianity is considered a "particularly serious threat" because it "provides a platform for social and political organization and interaction outside the realm of the State," according to the United Nations report.

Christians are barred from practicing their religion, and those caught doing so are "subject to severe punishments," the report found. North Korean leaders also conflate Christians with those detained in prison camps, those who try to flee and "others considered to introduce subversive influences," the report stated.

In interviews with The New York Times in 2012, four North Koreans said that they had been warned that the gulag awaited those who spoke to journalists or Christian missionaries. "If the government finds out I am reading the Bible, I'm dead," one woman said.

In its 2018 World Watch List, the Christian group Open Doors ranked North Korea the worst nation in the world for Christians, and in a statement last week, the group called on Christians to take part in 24 hours of prayer and fasting on Monday ahead of the meeting between Mr. Trump and Mr. Kim.

'DELIBERATE STARVATION' AS A PLAY FOR POWER

Two million to three million people were believed to have died during an extended famine in North Korea in the 1990s, The New York Times reported in 1999, around when the country began to recover.

At the time, North Korea used food as a tool to enforce political loyalty, prioritizing its distribution based on who was most useful to the nation's political system, the United Nations report stated.

More recently, the inmate population in North Korea's political prison camps has been culled through "deliberate starvation," the report found, adding that suspects are also starved "to increase the pressure on them to confess and to incriminate other persons."

When the 2014 report was conducted, it found that hunger and malnutrition were still widespread problems among the general population, and deaths from starvation continued to be reported.

That prompted the United Nations commission to raise concerns that another mass starvation could occur. "Laws and policies that violate the right to adequate food and freedom from hunger remain in place," the report said.

What Happened in the Trump-Kim Meeting and Why It Matters

BY MAX FISHER | JUNE 12, 2018

EVEN THE MOST informed observer might struggle to know what to make of the summit meeting between President Trump and Kim Jong-un of North Korea.

Colorful theatrics, such as a four-minute video that Mr. Trump showed Mr. Kim, gave the event an air of surrealism. Expectations ranged wildly, with Mr. Trump promising the deal of the century and many analysts fearing a blowup similar to what happened at last week's Group of 7 meeting in Canada.

And Mr. Trump's habit of making misleading statements, along with his record of defying norms, can make it difficult to parse which of the summit's outcomes matter and which don't, which bring Mr. Trump and Mr. Kim closer to their respective goals and which move them further away.

Here, then, is a simple breakdown of 10 major takeaways from the meeting and why they matter.

WHAT HAPPENED AND DIDN'T

(1) Almost any talks between the United States and North Korea, while those talks are continuing, significantly reduce the risk of an accidental or unintended slide into war, which could kill millions. The simple act of talking changes North Korean and American behaviors and perceptions in ways that make conflict far less likely. That's a big deal.

(2) The joint statement signed by Mr. Trump and Mr. Kim contains polite diplomatic platitudes but is otherwise largely empty. Among adversaries, this sort of statement is a common, low-pressure way to keep talks going. It doesn't resolve any issues, but it keeps the countries engaged.

(3) Later, Mr. Trump made a concession with significance that is real but easy to overstate: The United States will suspend its joint military exercises with South Korea. Mr. Trump was setting a policy that analysts refer to as "freeze for freeze," in which the United States freezes the exercises and North Korea freezes its weapons tests. It's meant to reduce tensions and create space for more meaningful concessions. Though not all analysts support such a policy, it is a mainstream idea and hardly radical.

(4) There is one asterisk to the otherwise modest policy implications. South Korean officials expressed surprise at Mr. Trump's promise to suspend joint military exercises, suggesting that Mr. Trump may have made the concession on South Korea's behalf without its consent or advance knowledge. The South Korean leadership will probably swallow their pride and accept it, but Mr. Trump's public breach of the alliance sends the message that South Koreans cannot always count on the United States. It also offers North Korea the tantalizing prospect of widening any divide between Washington and Seoul.

THE THEATER THAT MATTERED

(5) The United States staged the summit meeting in a way that handed Mr. Kim some symbolic but meaningful concessions. At the North Koreans' request, the two countries and their leaders were presented as equals — elevating Mr. Kim from global pariah to a superpower's peer. Their meeting was given pomp and ceremony at points verging on that of a royal wedding. Because Mr. Kim's legitimacy is among his greatest vulnerabilities at home and abroad, this staging was a big gift to him.

(6) It costs the United States little to make those concessions. Still, they can be given away only once, and the United States received relatively little from North Korea in return. Analysts broadly consider this a lost opportunity to extract more meaningful concessions from North Korea, such as partial disarmament or intrusive nuclear inspections.

(7) The meeting sends important messages to other adversarial states. Mr. Kim appears to have forced Mr. Trump to the table by developing nuclear weapons and missiles that can reach the United States. But Mr. Kim's human rights record, considered among the world's worst, did not appear to be an issue. Mr. Trump even suggested that North Korea could become a major tourist destination, almost exactly one year after an American tourist, Otto Warmbier, died of what appeared to be torture endured while in North Korean custody.

THE BIGGER PICTURE

(8) If the point of the meeting was to bring the world demonstrably closer to resolving the North Korea crisis, then that didn't happen. North Korea took no steps, even rhetorical, toward disarming. The United States also made no concrete, long-term changes; the freeze on exercises can be easily reversed. The meeting fell far short of Mr. Trump's lofty promises of North Korean denuclearization. But it also averted analysts' fears that Mr. Trump might make an outright withdrawal of American troops from South Korea or blow up at Mr. Kim.

(9) Mr. Trump's foreign policy actions elsewhere may limit what he can accomplish with North Korea. By tearing up the Iran nuclear deal despite sustained indication of Iranian compliance, and by reneging on agreements even with long-term allies, the United States has deepened suspicion that it cannot be trusted to make arms-control agreements. So don't expect talks to produce much of verifiable substance.

(10) Still, it's worth reiterating that first point: Almost any talks, even if they elevate Mr. Kim and grant him concessions for little return, significantly reduce the risk of war. The effect applies only as long as talks continue, so is almost certainly temporary. But as

Mr. Trump said in the joint news conference on Tuesday: “If I have to say I’m sitting on a stage with Chairman Kim and that’s going to get us to save 30 million lives, maybe more than that, I’m willing to sit on the stage. I’m willing to travel to Singapore very gladly.”

Kim Jong-un Says He Wants Denuclearization in Trump's Current Term

BY CHOE SANG-HUN | SEPT. 6, 2018

SEOUL, SOUTH KOREA — Offering an olive branch to President Trump, Kim Jong-un told a South Korean envoy that he wanted to denuclearize North Korea before Mr. Trump's current term ends in early 2021, the envoy said on Thursday.

Expressing frustration over what he called Washington's failure to negotiate in good faith, Mr. Kim told the envoy, Chung Eui-yong, that he still had confidence in Mr. Trump. He said he had never spoken badly of the American leader, even to his closest aides, since the two met in Singapore on June 12, according to Mr. Chung.

The president responded on Twitter early Thursday, expressing appreciation for Mr. Kim's "unwavering faith in President Trump." He added, "We will get it done together!"

Mr. Chung was sent by President Moon Jae-in of South Korea to Pyongyang, the North Korean capital, on Wednesday in hopes of reviving the stalled talks between the North and the United States over how to denuclearize North Korea. Mr. Moon plans to go to Pyongyang on Sept. 18 to meet with Mr. Kim and discuss improving the Koreas' relationship, including potential economic cooperation.

At a televised news conference in Seoul, Mr. Chung said Mr. Kim had voiced frustration that his commitment to nuclear disarmament, which he expressed when he met with Mr. Moon in April and with Mr. Trump in June, was not taken seriously by much of the world. Mr. Kim said that while North Korea had already taken important steps toward denuclearization, Washington was not doing enough in return, Mr. Chung said.

"He strongly expressed his will to take more active steps for denuclearization if the actions North Korea has already taken are matched by corresponding measures" from the United States, Mr. Chung said.

"He made it clear that his trust in President Trump remains — and will remain — unchanged, even though there have recently been some difficulties in negotiations between the North and the United States," Mr. Chung said. "He said he wished he could eliminate 70 years of hostile history with the United States, improve North Korea-U.S. relations and realize denuclearization within the first term of President Trump."

Mr. Chung said Mr. Kim gave him messages to relay to Washington, which officials said were being sent to his American counterpart, John Bolton, Mr. Trump's national security adviser. Mr. Chung did not reveal their contents, except to say that Mr. Kim wanted Washington's assurances that he had not made a mistake when he committed to the denuclearization of the Korean Peninsula.

Taken at face value, Mr. Kim's remarks, as relayed by the South Korean envoy, signaled that North Korea was willing to strike a denuclearization deal personally with Mr. Trump, who has been more eager to engage North Korea than any of his predecessors. They also suggested Mr. Kim could accept the rapid denuclearization the Trump administration has sought — for the right incentives.

The Singapore meeting made Mr. Trump the first sitting American president to meet with a North Korean leader. He has since boasted of his "warm" relationship with the dictator, who has test-launched missiles capable of reaching the continental United States and been accused of gruesome human rights abuses, including the summary executions of his uncle and other political enemies.

His administration has maintained a harder line. On Thursday, the Justice Department said it had charged a North Korean in the 2014 hacking of Sony Pictures Entertainment and accused the North of a broad conspiracy that caused hundreds of millions of dollars in losses worldwide.

Analysts said Mr. Kim was wooing Mr. Trump in hopes of dividing him from his hard-line advisers, in order to prevent the president from returning to the threats of military action that he made last year.

"Kim Jong-un is buying time," said Lee Byong-chul, a senior fellow at the Institute for Peace and Cooperation in Seoul. "He probably saw that there was nothing good in provoking Trump," especially when the American president "faces deepening legal trouble at home and disarray in his administration."

The North's state-run Korean Central News Agency said Mr. Kim had reaffirmed North Korea's commitment to denuclearize during his meetings with Mr. Chung. But it fell short of saying whether Mr. Kim would take major steps toward that goal.

Mr. Kim has not offered to provide a full inventory of nuclear weapons and fissile materials, as Washington has demanded. Nor has Mr. Kim offered any detailed plan for disarmament.

He also repeated his country's longstanding demand that denuclearization must include the removal of a "nuclear threat" to North Korea, a common reference to American military exercises in the region.

During their meeting in Singapore, Mr. Trump and Mr. Kim pledged to establish "new" relations and build "a lasting and stable peace regime," while Mr. Kim agreed to "work toward complete denuclearization" of the Korean Peninsula.

But their diplomats' negotiations have since stalled over differences on how to carry out that vaguely worded agreement. Mr. Trump, after boasting that he had largely resolved the North Korean nuclear crisis, abruptly canceled Secretary of State Mike Pompeo's planned visit to Pyongyang last week, citing a lack of progress in the denuclearization talks.

North Korea insists that it will move toward denuclearization only "in phases" and in exchange for "simultaneous" reciprocal concessions from Washington, a principle that Mr. Kim reiterated when he met with the South Korean envoy.

Mr. Chung said Mr. Kim brought up a series of confidence-building measures his country has taken this year, such as a moratorium on nuclear and missile tests, demolishing his country's only nuclear test site and dismantling a missile engine-test facility.

He said Mr. Kim objected to the skepticism that had greeted those actions in some quarters, such as the suspicion that North Korea could reactivate its nuclear test site. Mr. Kim said the underground site had been so thoroughly destroyed that no more tests could be carried out there. Mr. Kim also said the facility for testing missile engines was the only one in the North, and that its removal therefore meant a "complete halt to tests of long-range ballistic missiles," Mr. Chung said.

The most immediate reciprocal step North Korea wants from Washington is to declare an end to the Korean War, which was halted with an armistice in 1953.

But American officials fear that once such a declaration is made, North Korea will demand that the United States stop conducting joint military exercises with South Korea and withdraw its tens of thousands of troops based there.

Mr. Kim dismissed such concerns, saying that the declaration would "have nothing to do with" the South Korean-United States alliance or any withdrawal of American troops, Mr. Chung said.

Mr. Moon's spokesman said Thursday that Mr. Trump, in a recent conversation with Mr. Moon, had asked South Korea to be "chief negotiator" between the United States and North Korea. But Washington has also repeatedly warned South Korea against improving ties with Pyongyang without tangible progress toward denuclearization.

Lee Sung-yoon, a professor of Korean studies at Tufts University, said that in its eagerness to improve ties, South Korea was coddling the North and exaggerating its willingness to denuclearize. He said Mr. Chung would take "happy" messages from Pyongyang to the White House and argue that Mr. Trump "can do business with Kim."

Glossary

agitprop Political propaganda, often distributed through the arts.

armistice A temporary cessation of warfare between opponents.

axis of evil Phrase coined by U.S. President George W. Bush to describe foreign governments (initially Iran, Iraq, and North Korea) engaged in acts of terror or the development of nuclear weapons.

bonhomie Good-natured and friendly in nature.

communism A political and economic doctrine based on the teachings of Karl Marx in which goods are owned in common; a totalitarian system of government in which a sole party controls the state-owned means of production.

comprador capitalist Pejorative term for the leaders of a developing country in the early stages of capitalism who profit personally by acting to the benefit of foreign powers.

cult of personality A situation in which a single figure, often a political leader, is presented to a group of people as unquestionably worthy of absolute admiration and devotion.

denuclearization The process of removing nuclear arms and dismantling programs for their development.

erstwhile Formerly; in the past.

fete A lavish celebration or festivities.

generalissimo The chief commander of armed forces.

hagiography Biography of a saint or revered figure.

iconography The traditional images or icons associated with a figure, often religious or mythical.

indoctrination Instruction in a set of beliefs or principles, generally religious or political.

infallible Incapable of making errors or mistakes in the teaching of a religious or moral doctrine.

juche Korean word for "self-reliance" that denotes the official North Korean state ideology of Korean nationalism, self-reliance, and unwavering devotion to the leaders from the Kim family.

moratorium A cessation of activity.

Mount Paektu An active volcano along the border of North Korea and China that holds an important place in Korean mythology as the birthplace of Dangun, the legendary founder of the first Korean kingdom. It is also claimed to be the birthplace of Kim Jong-il.

nepotism Appointment to jobs or positions based on kinship.

rapprochement Establishment of peaceful diplomatic relations.

Supreme People's Assembly Legislative body of North Korea, consisting of one chamber of 687 deputies.

38th parallel The line of latitude used to divide the Korean peninsula, initially as a part of a joint strategy by the U.S.S.R. and the United States to liberate Korea from Japanese control, which served as the initial boundary between North and South Korea until the Korean War.

Media Literacy Terms

"Media literacy" refers to the ability to access, understand, critically assess and create media. The following terms are important components of media literacy, and they will help you critically engage with the articles in this title.

angle The aspect of a news story that a journalist focuses on and develops.

balance Principle of journalism that both perspectives of an argument should be presented in a fair way.

commentary A type of story that is an expression of opinion on recent events by a journalist generally known as a commentator.

credibility The quality of being trustworthy and believable, said of a journalistic source.

impartiality Principle of journalism that a story should not reflect a journalist's bias and should contain balance.

intention The motive or reason behind something, such as the publication of a news story.

interview story A type of story in which the facts are gathered primarily by interviewing another person or persons.

op-ed An opinion piece that reflects a prominent individual's opinion on a topic of interest.

reliability The quality of being dependable and accurate, said of a journalistic source.

tone A manner of expression in writing or speech.

Media Literacy Questions

1. Identify the various sources cited in the article "North Korean Leader Plans Huge Fete for Son" (on page 56). How does Henry Scott Stokes attribute information to each of these sources in the article? How effective are Stokes's attributions in helping the reader identify his sources?

2. In "Blurred Images of North Korea's 'Junior' " (on page 101), Elaine Sciolino directly quotes from the book "The True Story of Kim Jong-il." What are the strengths of the use of a direct quote from a book? What are the weaknesses?

3. Compare the headlines of "Kim Il-sung, Enigmatic 'Great Leader' of North Korea for 5 Decades, Dies at 82" (on page 86) and "Death Doesn't End Rule of Kim Il-sung, 'Eternal President' " (on page 95). Which is a more compelling headline, and why? How could the less compelling headline be changed to better draw the reader's interest?

4. What type of story is "Choosing The Right Enemies" (on page 124)? Can you identify another article in this collection that is the same type of story?

5. Does Motoko Rich demonstrate the journalistic principles of impartiality in her article "Trump and Kim Arrive in Singapore for Historic Summit Meeting" (on page 196)? If so, how did she do so? If not, what could she have included to make her article more impartial?

6. The article "The Obsessions of Kim Jong-il" (on page 127) is an example of an op-ed. Identify how B. R. Myers's attitude and tone help convey his opinion on the topic.

7. Does "The Last Emperor" (on page 130) use multiple sources? What are the strengths of using multiple sources in a journalistic piece? What are the weaknesses of relying heavily on one source or few sources?

8. What is the intention of the article "Visit Revises Image of North Korean" (on page 120)? How effectively does it achieve its intended purpose?

9. Analyze the authors' reporting in "Absolute Ruler of North Korea" (on page 47) and "To Sell a New Leader, North Korea Finds a Mirror Is Handy" (on page 172). Do you think one journalist is more balanced in their reporting than the other? If so, why do you think so?

10. Often, as a news story develops, a journalist's attitude toward the subject may change. Compare "Korean Leaders Meet in Pyongyang" (on page 152) and "Kim Jong-un's Image Shift: From Nuclear Madman to Skillful Leader" (on page 191), both by Choe Sang-Hun. Did new information discovered between the publication of these two articles change the journalist's perspective?

11. Identify each of the sources in "Kim Jong-Un's Claim of North Korea Hydrogen Bomb Draws Skepticism" (on page 188) as a primary source or a secondary source. Evaluate the reliability and credibility of each source. How does your evaluation of each source change your perspective on this article?

Citations

All citations in this list are formatted according to the Modern Language Association's (MLA) style guide.

BOOK CITATION

NEW YORK TIMES EDITORIAL STAFF, THE. *North Korea's Supreme Leaders: Kim Il-sung, Kim Jong-il and Kim Jong-un*. New York: New York Times Educational Publishing, 2019.

ONLINE ARTICLE CITATIONS

BOUC, ALAIN. "A Visit to North Korea." *The New York Times*, 14 Jun. 1971, https://www.nytimes.com/1971/06/14/archives/a-visit-to-north-korea.html.

BURNS, JOHN F. "The Kim Dynasty's North Korea: A Nation Centered on One Family." *The New York Times*, 9 Jul. 1985, https://www.nytimes.com/1985/07/09/world/the-kim-dynasty-s-north-korea-a-nation-centered-on-one-family.html.

CHIRA, SUSAN. "For North Korea, A Harsh Portrait." *The New York Times*, 23 Dec. 1988, https://www.nytimes.com/1988/12/23/world/for-north-korea-a-harsh-portrait.html.

FISHER, MAX. "What Happened in the Trump-Kim Meeting and Why It Matters." *The New York Times*, 12 Jun. 2018, https://www.nytimes.com/2018/06/12/world/asia/trump-kim-meeting-interpreter.html.

JOHNSTON, RICHARD J. H. "Communist Issue Growing in Korea." *The New York Times*, 27 Apr. 1946, https://www.nytimes.com/1946/04/27/archives/communist-issue-growing-in-korea-leader-from-soviet-zone-has.html.

KRISTOF, NICHOLAS D. "Death Doesn't End Rule of Kim Il-sung, 'Eternal President.' " *The New York Times*, 7 Sept. 1998, https://www.nytimes.com/1998/09/07/world/death-doesn-t-end-rule-of-kim-il-sung-eternal-president.html.

KRISTOF, NICHOLAS D. "Great Leader to Dear Leader." *The New York Times*, 20 Aug. 1989, https://www.nytimes.com/1989/08/20/magazine/great-leader-to-dear-leader.html.

KRISTOF, NICHOLAS D. "Inside the Mind of North Korea's 'Dear Leader': First, Pay Attention. And Then Pay Up." *The New York Times*, 6 Sept. 1998, https://www.nytimes.com/1998/09/06/weekinreview/world-inside-mind-north-korea-s-dear-leader-first-pay-attention-then-pay-up.html.

KRISTOF, NICHOLAS D. "North Korea's Favorite Son Wins Top Title." *The New York Times*, 9 Oct. 1997, https://www.nytimes.com/1997/10/09/world/north-korea-s-favorite-son-wins-top-title.html.

KRISTOF, NICHOLAS D. "North Koreans Officially Inherit Another 'Great Leader.' " *The New York Times*, 9 Oct. 1997, https://www.nytimes.com/1998/09/06/world/north-koreans-officially-inherit-another-great-leader.html.

LEE, JOHN M. "Absolute Ruler of North Korea." *The New York Times*, 31 May 1972, https://www.nytimes.com/1972/05/31/archives/absolute-ruler-of-north-korea-kim-il-sung.html.

MAASS, PETER. "The Last Emperor." *The New York Times*, 19 Oct. 2003, https://www.nytimes.com/2003/10/19/magazine/the-last-emperor.html.

MYERS, B. R. "The Obsessions of Kim Jong-il." *The New York Times*, 19 May 2003, https://www.nytimes.com/2003/05/19/opinion/the-obsessions-of-kim-jong-il.html.

THE NEW YORK TIMES. "Excerpts From Interview With North Korean Premier on Policy Toward the U.S." *The New York Times*, 31 May 1972, https://www.nytimes.com/1972/05/31/archives/excerpts-from-interview-with-north-korean-premier-on-policy-toward.html.

THE NEW YORK TIMES. "Korean Nationalist: Kim Il-sung." *The New York Times*, 24 Jan. 1968, https://www.nytimes.com/1968/01/24/archives/korean-nationalist-kim-il-sung.html.

THE NEW YORK TIMES. "North Korea Bids Reds Back Hanoi." *The New York Times*, 6 Oct. 1966, https://www.nytimes.com/1966/10/06/archives/north-korea-bids-reds-back-hanoi-premier-asks-them-to-send.html.

THE NEW YORK TIMES. "North Korea Head Calls Labor Lax." *The New York Times*, 25 Nov. 1949, https://www.nytimes.com/1949/11/25/archives/north-korea-head-calls-labor-lax-red-leader-says-workers-do-not.html.

THE NEW YORK TIMES. "North Korea Says the World Hails Kim Il-sung." *The New York Times*, 25 Nov. 1969, https://www.nytimes.com/1969/11/25

/archives/north-korea-says-the-world-hails-kim-il-sung-depicts-ads-for.html.

THE NEW YORK TIMES. "North Korean Enigma: Kim Il-sung." *The New York Times*, 12 Jul. 1961, https://www.nytimes.com/1961/07/12/archives/north-korean-enigma-kim-il-sung.html.

THE NEW YORK TIMES. "North Will Demand Rule of All Korea." *The New York Times*, 1 Sept. 1948, https://www.nytimes.com/1948/09/01/archives/north-will-demand-rule-of-all-korea.html.

THE NEW YORK TIMES. "Premier of North Tells Army to Fight to End Against U.N." *The New York Times*, 11 Oct. 1950, https://www.nytimes.com/1950/10/11/archives/premier-of-north-tells-army-to-fight-to-end-against-un-kim-in.html.

THE NEW YORK TIMES. "The 38th Parallel." *The New York Times*, 29 Sept. 1945, https://www.nytimes.com/1945/09/29/archives/the-38th-parallel.html.

THE NEW YORK TIMES. "War in Korea." *The New York Times*, 26 Jun. 1950, https://www.nytimes.com/1950/06/26/archives/war-in-korea.html.

O'HANLON, MICHAEL. "Choosing The Right Enemies." *The New York Times*, 6 Feb. 2002, https://www.nytimes.com/2002/02/06/opinion/choosing-the-right-enemies.html.

PERLEZ, JANE. "Visit Revises Image of North Korean." *The New York Times*, 26 Oct. 2000, https://www.nytimes.com/2000/10/26/world/visit-revises-image-of-north-korean.html.

POLLACK, ANDREW. "Mourning for North Korea Leader Ends, but Son Is Not Anointed." *The New York Times*, 9 Jul. 1997, https://www.nytimes.com/1997/07/09/world/mourning-for-north-korea-leader-ends-but-son-is-not-anointed.html.

POLLACK, ANDREW. "North Korea's Heir Apparent Meets Foreign Diplomats." *The New York Times*, 12 Jul. 1994, https://www.nytimes.com/2002/12/03/world/a-telling-north-korean-journey.html.

RICH, MOTOKO. "Trump and Kim Arrive in Singapore for Historic Summit Meeting." *The New York Times*, 10 Jun. 2018, https://www.nytimes.com/2018/06/10/world/asia/kim-jong-un-trump-north-korea-singapore.html.

SALAM, MAYA, AND MATTHEW HAAG. "Atrocities Under Kim Jong-un: Indoctrination, Prison Gulags, Executions." *The New York Times*, 11 Jun. 2018, https://www.nytimes.com/2018/06/11/world/asia/north-korea-human-rights.html.

SALISBURY, HARRISON E. "Premier's Presence Blankets Pyongyang." *The New York Times*, 17 May 1972, https://www.nytimes.com/1972/05/17/archives/premiers-presence-blankets-pyongyang.html.

SANGER, DAVID E. "For the Great Leader at 80, a Great Birthday Bash." *The*

New York Times, 11 May 1992, https://www.nytimes.com/1992/05/11/world/pyongyang-journal-for-the-great-leader-at-80-a-great-birthday-bash.html.

SANGER, DAVID E. "Kim Il-sung, Enigmatic 'Great Leader' of North Korea for 5 Decades, Dies at 82." *The New York Times*, 10 Jul. 1994, https://www.nytimes.com/1994/07/10/obituaries/death-leader-kim-il-sung-enigmatic-great-leader-north-korea-for-5-decades-dies.html.

SANGER, DAVID E. "Kim Jong-il, Dictator Who Turned North Korea Into a Nuclear State, Dies." *The New York Times*, 18 Dec. 2011, https://www.nytimes.com/2011/12/19/world/asia/Kim-Jong-il-Dictator-Who-Turned-North-Korea-Into-a-Nuclear-State-Dies.html.

SANGER, DAVID E. "U.S. Confronts Consequences of Underestimating North Korean Leader." *The New York Times*, 24 Apr. 2014, https://www.nytimes.com/2014/04/25/world/asia/wrong-guesses-about-north-korea-leave-us-struggling-to-adjust.html.

SANG-HUN, CHOE. "At Huge Rally, North Koreans Declare Kim Their Leader." *The New York Times*, 29 Dec. 2011, https://www.nytimes.com/2011/12/30/world/asia/north-korea-declares-kim-jong-un-as-supreme-leader.html.

SANG-HUN, CHOE. "Kim Jong-un Says He Wants Denuclearization in Trump's Current Term." *The New York Times*, 09 Sept. 2018, https://www.nytimes.com/2018/09/06/world/asia/kim-jong-un-donald-trump-denuclearize.html.

SANG-HUN, CHOE. "Kim Jong-un's Claim of North Korea Hydrogen Bomb Draws Skepticism." *The New York Times*, 10 Dec. 2015, https://www.nytimes.com/2015/12/11/world/asia/north-korea-kim-hydrogen-bomb.html.

SANG-HUN, CHOE. "Kim Jong-un's Image Shift: From Nuclear Madman to Skillful Leader." *The New York Times*, 6 Jun. 2018, https://www.nytimes.com/2018/06/06/world/asia/kim-korea-image.html.

SANG-HUN, CHOE. "Korean Leaders Meet in Pyongyang." *The New York Times*, 2 Oct. 2007, https://www.nytimes.com/2007/10/02/world/asia/02cnd-korea.html.

SANG-HUN, CHOE. "North Korea Takes Steps to Extend Dynastic Rule." *The New York Times*, 2 Sept. 2010, https://www.nytimes.com/2010/09/03/world/asia/03nkorea.html.

SANG-HUN, CHOE. "North Korea Tries to Show Its Leader Is Healthy and in Control." *The New York Times*, 6 Nov. 2008, https://www.nytimes.com/2008/11/07/world/asia/07kim.html.

SANG-HUN, CHOE. "North Korean Leader Stresses Need for Strong Military." *The New York Times*, 15 Apr. 2012, https://www.nytimes.com/2012/04/16/world/asia/kim-jong-un-north-korean-leader-talks-of-military-superiority

-in-first-public-speech.html.

SANG-HUN, CHOE. "To Sell a New Leader, North Korea Finds a Mirror Is Handy." *The New York Times*, 1 Feb. 2012, https://www.nytimes.com/2012/02/02/world/asia/packaging-of-Kim-Jong-un-in-north-korea.html.

SANG-HUN, CHOE, AND DAVID E. SANGER. "North Korea's Leader Is Said to Oust Uncle in Power Play." *The New York Times*, 3 Dec. 2013, https://www.nytimes.com/2013/12/04/world/asia/uncle-of-north-korean-leader-stripped-of-power-according-to-reports.html.

SCIOLINO, ELAINE. "Blurred Images of North Korea's 'Junior.' " *The New York Times*, 17 Jul. 1994, https://www.nytimes.com/1994/07/17/world/blurred-images-of-north-korea-s-junior.html.

STOKES, HENRY SCOTT. "North Korean Leader Plans Huge Fete for Son." *The New York Times*, 17 March 1982, https://www.nytimes.com/1982/03/17/world/north-korean-leader-plans-huge-fete-for-son.html.

STOKES, HENRY SCOTT. "Son of North Korean Leader Taking a New Step Up." *The New York Times*, 10 Aug. 1980, https://www.nytimes.com/1980/08/10/archives/son-of-north-korean-leader-taking-a-new-step-up-some-believe-power.html.

Index

This book is current up until the time of printing. For the most up-to-date reporting, visit www.nytimes.com.